THE PROPHETIC
CHURCH IN THE PUBLIC FORUM

A TIME TO
SPEAK

RAY CLEARY

COVENTRY
PRESS

Published in Australia by
Coventry Press
33 Scoresby Road
Bayswater VIC 3153

ISBN 9781922589057

Scripture quotations are from *Revised Standard Version Bible*, © 1989 Division of Christian Education of the National Council of the Churches of Christ in the United States of America. Used by permission, All rights reserved.

Catalogue-in-Publication entry is available from the National Library of Australia
http://catalogue.nla.gov.au

Cover design by Ian James – www.jgd.com.au
Cover photograph by Patrick Perkins on Unsplash
Text design by Coventry Press
Typeset in Tex Gyre Pagella

Printed in Australia

Contents

Introduction   5

1. Failures of the Churches   11

2. Privatisation and Marginalisation of Faith   18

3. Australia in a Changing World   25

4. Justice   33

5. Justice and the Anglican Tradition   36

6. The Prophets   42

7. Justice and Moses and Jesus   47

8. The Decline of the Church's Prophetic Voice   53

9. The Churches' Vocation of Social Justice   59

10. How the Church Can Speak in Context   62

11. Reclaiming a Prophetic Voice   71

12. Where to Now?   76

13. Challenges   83

Conclusions   93

Bibliography   100

A Church that does not provoke any crisis, preach a Gospel that does not unsettle, proclaim a word of God that does not get under anyone's skin, or the word of God that does not touch the real sin of the society in which it is being proclaimed: what kind of Gospel is that? – Oscar Romero

Introduction

The purpose of this short book is to explore and address the question of how the Church – or more accurately, churches – in Australia should engage in the public forum of ideas and hopes for community life, and in shaping what it means to be human, created in the image of God. This piece of writing and reflection is not meant to be an academic book but rather a narrative of issues and concerns that need to be addressed if the Christian Church is to survive and influence the life of people across the world in building just and compassionate communities irrespective of gender, race, ethnicity, status or intelligence. It argues the need for listening deeply to others, building connections, and a renewed vision of mission that is contemporary and authentic, optimistic about the future of the Church, and respectful of the right to dissent and disagree. Respectful dialogue and engagement with those who may differ or express their faith differently also need to be valued and acknowledged.

The book stems in part from my own frustration that the contribution that churches have made to Australian society is often misrepresented, summarily dismissed, and that, as Christians, we seem oblivious to the reasons why, and therefore act as though nothing has really changed. Further, it challenges those who seek to expunge Christian faith from the public arena and is a reminder to those who exercise leadership in the churches to engage in respectful and meaningful conversation with all who seek to shame, abuse, denigrate and challenge those who speak about injustice at all levels of community.

This is a time when there are significant internal divisions and disputes within churches of different traditions and denominations on matters of Scripture, doctrine and structure as well as the range of emerging social and ethical issues unknown in biblical times. Ecclesiastical, clerical and patriarchal leadership is also under question from the laity and, in particular, women. One such outcome is a weakened ecumenical voice. Another is the lack of agreement within denominations on key ethical and faith matters. Women have felt marginalised in decision-making and leadership roles. As a result, new barriers have emerged that have diminished the ability of the churches to be heard with clarity, consistency and uniformity. While there is a view that the Church as an institution is in decline, even this is confusing, as there is no such entity as the Church but rather churches, and then a number of what can be best described as parachurches that make up the broad Christian community.

There is a broader perception by many in our community that the Church's agenda is to conceal, to control the lives of ordinary men and women, and to create society more in its own image, or in a particular doctrine that denies the full humanity of women and others who do not fit its stereotyped view. Many see the Church as concerned more about its own survival than God's mission. In simple terms, the narrative of the churches is seen no longer to fit or to offer anything to improve the human condition. I am not suggesting that this widely-held view that exists in Australian society is true, but there are many elements that I will explore further that do have credence.

A further reason for writing is the author's deeply held belief that the Christian narrative has important things to say about what it means to be human in today's world and about the role of civil society in Australia and in the global context. Another reason is that much of our secular society has strong, deep theological roots that we ignore or are in danger of losing, as the full impact of neoliberalism takes control of our social and economic lives, throwing out the historical role of the state as an instrument of compassion, sharing and justice.

While Christian faith may not provide all the immediate answers to the social, economic and ethical issues of our day, we should not assume that the secular, humanist option is better. Communities and governments at all levels are increasingly fragile and requiring strong, compassionate and just leadership, not merely ideologically bound, unable to see or appreciate the challenges that face the global community, pursuing self-interest and giving lip service to those whose lives are a struggle.

There are other aspects of the Church's life that are fruitful and enduring. Equally, I have discovered in my own ministry over forty years that there is a latent hope in many people across all generations for a faith perspective that is more than self-centered and privileged, but, rather, expresses an understanding of the meaning and purpose of life that involves awe, mystery, transcendence and fulfilment. In this broader expression of hope and faith, institutional membership is rapidly in decline and rejected, while the search for spiritual integrity and connection continues and is found in emerging groups such as Common Grace and Planetshakers.

The challenges faced by the mainstream denominations are many and require a new way of reflecting on the way to reengage with the wider community. This agenda must involve listening as well as speaking, in order to hear the struggles, concerns and experiences of life of the community. This voice must acknowledge advances in knowledge across many disciplines and in particular science and technology. The church's message in response to new forms of knowledge must embrace liberation from the chains that shackle life to a way of being that is positive and creative.

Churches across Australia are present in every community and although under pressure in urban areas, in many rural places they remain, while banks, bakeries, post offices and police have left and consolidated in regional centres. The ongoing presence of churches in these areas provides an enduring opportunity, notwithstanding the challenges. New ways of thinking and action are required.

I am not a cradle Anglican, nor did I attend an Anglican, or any church-sponsored, school. My parents could not afford the fees, nor as nominal Christians, did they see any point in doing so. I am aware, however, that the fact that I did not attend one of the leading Melbourne Anglican schools, and throughout my life was an advocate for the public-school system, was to my disadvantage in the eyes of some in the Church and in the Melbourne Diocese. I did attend a major state secondary school where the pursuit of sport and academic achievement were the highest goals. Religion was discouraged by many of the staff except for the 30-minute religious education assembly each month. These assemblies were also often a great embarrassment. Nor was there any commitment to them by the school principal or staff. On many occasions, religion was openly ridiculed by the school leadership; and the cadet core scene and sport were of greater importance.

I did, however, attend from my mid-teens an Anglican Catholic parish where social justice, outreach to the community and beautiful worship went hand-in-hand. It was in this parish community that a respected priest taught me how to read the Scriptures in both the context of the time of its writing and in today's world. He was often challenged and criticised for his willingness to open the Scriptures to study and scrutiny. It was during this period that I began to learn how the revelation of God in Christ is an ongoing journey. Hence, my understanding of God has continued to change over the years.

1

Failures of the Churches

OW SHOULD THE CHURCH ENGAGE with society with integrity and transparency in expressing the unconditional love and deep concern that God has for the whole of Creation? This may seem an odd claim at a time when the churches are much in the news but, alas, for many of the wrong reasons. While it is true that church attendance in Australia has been falling for at least five to six decades, recent times have seen accelerated decline in a number of the mainstream churches, while new extroverted and Bible-based or parachurches have grown, and even exist within some of the mainstream denominations.

Younger people have been increasingly attracted to these expressions of church even though the churches' theology is often conservative in nature on matters of gender roles and human sexuality, while radical on matters such as climate change. This faith framework identifies closely with the so-called Prosperity Gospel, while on matters of personal moral ethics they are conservative. Only time will tell whether these models of faith will be maintained as young people grow and develop on the life journey.

On most of these issues, these churches are counter to the views of an increasingly secularised, wider Australian community, including a fading communal morality of compassion and justice replaced by self and economics. In the context of a drifting and changing morality, the more conservative faith expressions are louder and stronger than the mainstream churches.

I am an Anglican by faith tradition, and this has heavily influenced my writing and thoughts. Anglicans, in my own experience, are diverse in their theology, engaged in the political arena, ethically challenging, and regularly at loggerheads with one another. I suspect this dynamic context is one that I like and feel at home in, although from time to time I find it exasperating. As a teenager growing up in the Anglican faith tradition, there seemed to be more harmony, in spite of differences and a willingness to differ with less aggression between those who named themselves High Church and others Low Church. Both were regarded as legitimate expressions of Anglicanism and faithful to the *Book of Common Prayer*. In recent years, difference has accelerated into open feuds around issues of human sexuality and how the sacred Scriptures should be read and understood. Without doubt, this has contributed to the changed place of the Church in community and caused considerable hurt and embarrassment to many, both inside and outside the Church.

The motivation and energy for this book has come from many conversations with faithful Christians both lay and ordained who are experiencing a crisis of faith. Some have already abandoned the Church, but not necessarily faith and belief, while others are considering leaving the Church, dismayed by the lack of prophetic and liberating leadership and discernment at many different levels within faith communities. Others are distraught because of the leadership's attitudes – including that of local clergy – to human rights, gender and justice, and in their protection of church privilege. Others argue that moral and professional standards, governance and structural requirements go beyond the needs of the churches as the 'Body of Christ' and are an overreaction by hierarchical leadership in response to past failures and neglect. While not all leaders are in denial about the need for change, they feel powerless to influence the new requirements, unsure of how to move forward and feel sidelined in the discussions.

Many clergy and lay people feel a sense of powerlessness and despair in the light of revelations of abuses and cover-ups, as well as the rapid changes taking place in civil society. In many places, clergy and laity with a robust and enduring faith feel ill-equipped to meet the challenges of today. Many feel frustrated by what they describe as second order issues that continue to cause distress and disenchantment in the wider community regarding the churches' role. Many of the faithful are 'fed up', in the words of one parishioner, with the failure of the churches to get their act together.

This book is further based on the view – offered by Walter Brueggemann and others – that the Church is now in the wilderness, in exile, a remnant, estranged from the community in which it previously played a pivotal role. The voices of church leaders, once respected and listened to on many social and ethical issues, are now often ignored, misunderstood, challenged and not even reported in mainstream media. Church moderators and archbishops struggle not only to be heard but are not given the opportunity to speak and engage. When they are reported in the mainstream media, it is often in a negative and off-putting manner, the tone of the reporting and the headline a distraction from the message.

Religious leaders have been seen as covering up abuse of children by clergy and church workers, by condoning domestic violence and by failing to respond with compassion and justice to many social and economic matters that have the outcome of diminishing social cohesion and allowing power to be exercised by the wealthy and privileged at the expense of the majority. Often the responses of church leaders to their own failures have lacked substance and are seen as insensitive and out of touch with current thinking, particularly in the areas of personal morality, even if much of this criticism is in hindsight and does not reflect community attitudes at the time offences were committed. There are growing numbers that believe that the churches are privileged, like politicians and corporations, part of the ruling class, and, until recent times, untouchable and unaccountable.

If there is a church voice today, it is consistently limited to the more evangelical and fundamentalist churches, whether mainstream or parachurch, often described as the religious right, that advocate prosperity and salvation as central theological principles – that in the acceptance of Jesus as personal saviour all will be well. This form of theology is aligned with free-market, neoliberalist ideology. For some, this interpretation of Christian Scripture is attractive, emphasising well-being based on self-interest, and creating divisions between the deserving and undeserving, whom they interpret as lazy, maladjusted and ignorant. Their voice and approach undermine those who are struggling with life, blaming them for their situation and reflecting little of the compassion of a God who loves all unconditionally. Journalists fail to challenge these claims out of their own ignorance of the breadth of Christian teaching and for the sake of a cheap headline.

One of the major issues confronting the Church relates to the role of women. Many who seek to address issues of abuse and violence against women speak of the patriarchal society in which we live as being undergirded by religious teaching that places women in a subservient role to men. This is a particularly strong accusation against the Roman Catholic Church and some Protestant and parachurch groups who deny women a full role in Christian leadership and in marriage. The churches have been slow to respond to the secular and religious calls to embrace more fully the leadership of women. Conservative and more fundamentalist religious groups in Australia also disapprove of same-sex relationships.

Another area of major concern for many women and children in our community, and to a lesser extent, men – although they are the main perpetrators – is domestic violence. The Church, alongside the law and other institutions, has turned a blind eye to these occurrences and failed to hear the cries of pain and humiliation. Historically, many clergy advised women to return to abusive relationships while others reminded women they were to submit to their husbands in all manners. Similarly, the Church has not always dealt positively with our treatment of indigenous people and recently-arrived ethnic groups.

The mainstream churches are also divided on matters of the essentials of faith and the question of religious freedom and freedom of speech. The centre of Christian faith that teaches God as love, unconditional love, has been replaced by second or third order issues based on dogma and doctrine. These developed at a different time in history and fail to address the issues of today that require new ways of thinking and addressing what it means to be created in the image of God. New ways of thinking need to embrace the reality of the times and acknowledge that the era of Christendom in the West as it has been previously practised and presented is over.

The churches also need to note that there is no single religious framework that today provides a basis for communal living. Rather, as Jonathan Sacks says in his book *Not in God's Name*, ethical behaviour is based on a common humanity:

> Love your neighbour. Love the stranger. Hear the cry of the otherwise unloved. Liberate the poor from their poverty. Care for the dignity of all. Let those who have more than they need share their blessings with those who have less. Feed the hungry, house the homeless, and heal the sick in body and mind. Fight injustice, whoever it is done by and whoever it is done against. And do these things because, being human, we are bound by a covenant of human solidarity, whatever our colour or culture, class or creed.[1]

Sacks claims that these moral principles are increasingly being forgotten in free societies such as Australia. They are, I would add, forgotten also in parts of the Church. As governments increasingly abandon their commitment to all citizens, public trust has declined towards politicians, corporate, professional and religious leaders. Divisions between the have and have nots, changing gender roles, workplace reforms, advances in technology and living standards have all altered the nature of our humanity and sense of communal concern. As a result, people feel dejected, have lost hope and act according to the emotional and survival needs of the moment. This has resulted in the success of more extreme political expressions and a breakdown in social harmony. The 'me is now more important than the we'. The focus on my rights as more important than anything else is now a worrying trend in many democracies.

---

[1] Jonathan Sacks, *Not in God's Name: Confronting Religious Violence*, London: Hodder and Stoughton, 2015.

Sadly, churches have not been spared this lack of concern for the other. To the contrary, in order to protect their once privileged position, some churches are advocating for the right to discriminate in employment matters against those who do not hold their beliefs, in schools, hospitals and welfare agencies they auspice or manage. Many of these, however, are not strictly religious bodies but are public benevolent institutions. Others were created by acts of parliament. All receive substantial government (taxpayer) funds to carry out their work and accept the state's responsibility to provide service for all people irrespective of religion. This contradiction is not acknowledged by some churches who believe that in the current political climate, they have the advantage still in convincing government to protect their privileged position and to endorse conservative policies that reflect a growing distance between the community at large and church doctrine.

2

Privatisation and Marginalisation of Faith

THIS IS NOT THE FIRST TIME the Church has been in exile, persecuted or challenged. But the current failures of churches to observe their own teachings, be transparent, and to listen to the voices of those discriminated against or ignored in Australian life, namely the marginalised and those struggling to survive, have brought new dimensions to the present challenges. As a result, in many churches, faith has been privatised and personalised, and policies are put in place to protect their own members.

Justice and welfare obligations have been privatised with varying degrees of church or faith connections. Many church agencies are so in name only as they become increasingly an arm of government, with little if any mission objectives that reflect Christian compassion and justice. Nor are they intimately related to their local faith and broader communities.

In many ways, churches and faith are just another commodity that individuals can accept or reject in the same way as any other products. As a result, the churches' broad mission to shape and influence society has diminished. New regulations and requirements to implement safe practices have been time-consuming for leadership and parish administration and a major ongoing challenge. In some places, churches have withdrawn from community participation and into themselves, while others have taken on a role of protector of their own beliefs, with safeguarding their tradition as the first order and the only way to enable the building of the community of God here on earth.

I have highlighted the failure of the Church in the area of sexual abuse, but this is not the only reason for their reputation damage. There are many reasons for this shift, including the growth in technology, rising educational standards and increasing secularism. Previously in Australia, the Church's voice on matters such as industrial relations, education, housing, the basic wage, pensions and benefits and support for workers to increase their share of the common wealth was commonly heard and was seen as part of the churches' role to engage with society and pursue justice for all.

No longer is this the fact. Today, many statements by church leaders in the areas of personal morality, particularly human sexuality and the understanding of marriage, show how far the community has moved on from the influence of Christian faith, and church leaders' words create further distance and even embarrassment at times. Why the churches seem fixated on matters of human sexuality remains a mystery, although their attitudes are consistent with those of other faiths. However loud and disrespectful the voices of some church leaders are on matters of personal morality, they are often absent in the traditional areas of social justice. Lay Christians appear to have taken up the role with action and words while religious leaders are often silent.

In schools that are sponsored or owned by churches, the provision of education for the poor is a distant memory, other than a few scholarships, with the exception of the

Roman Catholic Church where faith and a commitment to justice still prevail. Other mainstream churches offer high quality education with faith and religion marginalised in their curriculum. The fees necessary to attend these schools means that parents who wish a faith education for their children must both work, while others are excluded because they are unable to pay the fees. Sunday schools as free schools for the poor is also a distant memory.

Faith-based schools and agencies of relief were in the past led and staffed by people of faith, giving them a legitimate and practical way of voicing concerns for the poor and disadvantaged. Faith provided the grounding for the agencies' purpose, a basis for participation in the public forum and in the provision of service. Sadly, for many agencies and schools today, this voice has been lost as they have been integrated into broader education and welfare programs using government funds, while losing their voice on crucial issues that demand action and their own mission. At the same time, fewer services are now actually run by the government but have been outsourced to the traditional church agencies. The outcome has been to silence their prophetic voice on social and ethical issues and compromise their mission. Whoever pays the piper calls the tune.

The influence of scientific knowledge has played a major role in reducing the place of religion in our contemporary world. From the days of the Enlightenment, when many challenges to religion from a scientific perspective began to emerge, to the present, science has in many places replaced answers that were once the domain of faith.

Science has enhanced the wellbeing of our community. The advances in science and medical technology have changed life expectancy, enabled birth control, liberated sexuality and helped explain aspects of life's mystery. It has also helped shape much theological and biblical teaching. Science and technology bring new dimensions to our understanding of sacred text and what it means to be human. Science and religion are complementary not protagonists, but some churches have reacted negatively to these advances by arguing that because these traditional sacred texts are the inspired word of God, they are unending and unchanging, resisting criticism or interpretation. Others re-interpret Scripture if it challenges traditional church doctrinal positions.

No major media outlet, other than the ABC in Australia, now has a specialist religious affair's reporter or department. As a result, religious matters and reports on faith in the secular media often appear with little if any understanding of the historical role and place of religion in the life of the community. Journalists appear to have neither the time nor interest to fully understand the influence of the Judaic Christian traditions and their underpinning of much of the values of western society. They tend to reflect the attitude of much of the wider community of a disinterest in religious or faith matters.

The fact that children no longer attend church in any form and Christian education is now absent from most public schools in Australia means a lack of any religious understanding that may help shape and influence discussion in the media. I recall many years ago being approached by a radio station about hot cross buns being on sale straight after Christmas. I responded by saying that I thought it was inappropriate but continued by saying that Christian faith had more to say than simply commenting on the premature sale of buns.

Many of the announcements by church leaders on social and ethical issues are at odds with the political and cultural agendas being set and pursued by the media and other groups.

Much of the churches' responses to these issues remains within their own catchments and do not see the light of day elsewhere. Unfortunately, many churches appear not to comprehend or understand the complexity of the issues and the significant changes that have occurred.

There are, from time to time, exceptions. In November 2019, the public announcement by the Anglican Bishop of the Riverina in New South Wales on climate change, the drought and the shortage of water affecting the farming communities in his diocese, and the current role of buying water by multinational companies, was timely and appropriate, and was widely reported. He spoke into the context and to the reality of the pain and suffering being experienced, and not from texts of dogma. This is mission at the coal face without judgment or moralising. There is an urgent need for similar responses to issues such as climate change, asylum seekers and refugees to be at the forefront of statements from religious leaders. This is not to suggest that the churches should always agree with those who hold different views but rather to reinforce the need for respectful dialogue and conversation.

Christian mission embraces proclamation, adoration and service. The highest expression of faith is to live love in service for the other as Jesus did throughout his ministry. This is a recurring theme throughout this book. I am regularly challenged by my non-churchgoing friends – many previously devout and committed to the faith – who voice anger, disappointment and despair about institutional church life as described and presented in the everyday social and main stream media.

Avenues of social media need to be utilised by church leaders to speak not only to their own constituents but to the wider community, and in order not to rely on mainstream media, who, while claiming independence and balance in news reporting, often fall far short of their own objective. But social media such as Facebook and Twitter are also used by thousands of Christians to express their views on issues affecting the world and at home. Different viewpoints and disagreement appear, showing diversity of belief among the faithful that challenges leaders.

The implication is clear. The traditional respect given to religious leaders has diminished and traditional forms of communication are failing. As the community continues to become more broadly educated and informed, challenge to patriarchal authority, perceived or otherwise, will invariably grow.

In his book *Dominion*, Tom Holland, an acclaimed English historian, writes about how Christianity has influenced the shape of Western Society, including humanism, secularism and agnosticism, noting that many are unaware of this fact. By his own admission, Holland is not a person of faith but values the contribution that Christianity has made to Western democracy. But he goes on to say that the Christian ethic of love and compassion for the other has now moved from being normal to being an option, and fading fast; and neoliberalism and a privatisation agenda is dominant, pushed by powerful media and corporate executives for their own interests. While neoliberalism has fueled economic growth and helped millions escape dismal poverty in poorer parts of the world, it has also created new poverty in many affluent Western countries such as the United States and Britain, where the gulf between rich and poor has grown wider. Greed, self-interest, discrimination, automation of the workforce, and lower taxes are all examples of how oligarchs have imposed their will on governments.

The Kingdom values of concern for the widow, the homeless and the common good have been replaced by homophobia, exclusion, discrimination and anti-environmentalism, not only as the centre pieces of corporate life but also of the Prosperity religion discussed earlier. Many within the mainstream churches who voice opposing views have been silenced and ignored by mainstream media and the religious hierarchies themselves. But for the Christian, the Cross should be a sign of protest against sin, violence, injustice and death. It speaks of 'love your enemy' and unconditional welcome, and challenges words of revenge, self-interest, wealth accumulation, ideology and power.

The Christian understanding of sin and all that separates us from God has been lost on most of Australian society and is no longer accepted as the standard for moral and ethical behavior. This is to not to say that the Church has always got it right. A brief reading of history will confirm otherwise, in the Church's attitudes to sexuality, the role of women, human rights and the care of the poor. Christian faith has not always liberated people from bondage, but rather the reverse. 'Father' has not always known best and still appears to struggle in many quarters. Communities of faith have contributed to this by placing clergy and religious leaders on a pedestal, failing to recognise their humanity and brokenness as equal to their own. Australian society, therefore, is at a new place in history, and previous assumptions about the role and place of Christianity as the determining influence in shaping who we are and what it means to be human is no longer relevant.

3

Australia in a Changing World

I n Australia, the changes in context and culture of the 1960s were the beginnings of a shifting place of the Church in community life. The shift has not been limited to Australia but has been occurring for many years in various places across the globe and in particular Europe and now in the United States. In contrast, in Africa, China, Asia and South America, the same trends are in reverse. Ethnic groups that have arrived from these communities in Australia in the main tend to continue their faith practices. This has led to the development of ethnic-specific congregations that in practice tend to be more theologically conservative. Their arrivals have in part camouflaged the decline in church attendance and adherence of the rest of the Australian population. As Gary Bouma said in his report to the Melbourne Diocese in 2013, 'Once part of the British empire, Anglicans and British Protestants have long had an international presence and taken a global view of history and economic development'. This, he says, has now changed.

The following discussions describe and illustrate the changes that have taken place not only in Australia but globally. Many of these changes explain the numerical decline in Sunday worship attendance and the voice of the Church in contemporary society. Many are outside the immediate influence of the Church. Covid 19 has further shown the cracks in Australian society that have arisen over the past forty years from the impact of short-term contract and casual work arrangements, rapid urbanisation and a declining rural sector where young people migrate to the city for employment and lifestyle.

We have seen the emergence of the 24/7 working and shopping week as a result of growing global population, and global free markets. The philosophy behind the free market is a neoliberal concern for one's own wellbeing first and then a trickle down of what is spare. The common good has been rapidly changing to mean the self good. Self-interest and ideology appear at the top of priorities for many political and corporate leaders. Recent reports claim that 380 billionaires across the world now own and control 50% of the globe's resources.

This was not always the approach of Australian governments, until the Hawke-Keating era, with the deregulations of the exchange rate and a privatisation agenda. Many of us were seduced by personality politics at the time while critical analysis was left to the few. It is true that there were initial benefits but time has shown that, without strong regulation, many of the initiatives have illusory, abused, manipulated and exploited for personal gain at the expense of the consumer. Service quality in many sectors has declined and there have been corporate insurance abuses and failures by financial institutions. The current support for increased gas exploration to feed a growing world market is seen as more important than investing in sustainable and renewable energy. In recent times, the crusade to have balanced federal budgets has been achieved by underspending in budget approved funding and to increasingly push for the privatisation of health and education services at the cost of public provisions.

Many services including government owned banks were privatised along with utilities including gas and electricity, much of this in the name of shareholder and executive bonuses and benefits. The loss of values of a shared humanity and state responsibility to ensure all were housed have been perhaps an unintended consequence. As a result, society has changed and many of the teachings associated with Christian faith – of concern for the wellbeing of others – increasingly appeared irrelevant to many.

The advent of Donald Trump and other more extreme right-wing conservative and neoliberal politicians elected to power across the world has changed the dynamics of international relationships including the free movement of trade and increased global tensions exacerbated in recent times by Covid 19. News reporting lacking accuracy and authenticity in mainstream media alongside social media outlets have corrupted truth. There is growing despair and anxiety across the globe. Many commentators fear the heart of democracy is being corrupted and destroyed as personal liberties are restricted and violence failed to be called out and outlawed. The rise of China and India further challenges the previous dominance of the United States and other western countries while the instability of Middle Eastern countries remains.

In Australia, policies to prevent asylum seekers and refugees settling here, along with the demand for lower immigration targets, are encouraged with the argument that immigrants take Australian jobs. This does not, however, prevent corporations outsourcing Australian jobs to foreign countries to reduce costs. Slogans like 'Make America Great Again', 'Britain for Britain' and 'Don't take Australian jobs' have grown. At the same time as Christian faith is being increasingly dismissed or ignored in the West, Islam is increasing its presence in many parts of the world, underpinning and enabling a renewed conservative moral code that influences political processes.

The impact of the internet and social media has widened community views. Twenty-four-hour news coverage has expanded the knowledge base for people across the nation with religious confrontations within and between religious traditions noted and digested. New barriers within and between churches has diminished ecumenism. This has affected how people view and understand faith and belief across the religious spectrum. Intelligent questions are asked about the place of religion as central to a person's life, and in many cases the churches response to these important life questions is seen to be inadequate for contemporary western society. One example is the issue of the sanctity of life and the place of suffering. This is a complicated issue and, unfortunately, the commitment to the sanctity of life by the Church has meant a failure to understand those who experience uncontrollable suffering.

Traditional service provision by churches since the mid 1980's particularly in Victoria, including kindergartens, youth programs, community meeting points and schools, which gave the Church the opportunity to engage the community, are now increasingly being provided by local councils and sporting clubs, placing the church further on the outside. The changes in Victoria to the provision of religious education in schools reflect changing community attitudes to belief and faith. Churches are increasingly having their privilege and power base challenged, partly in response to some churches using religious education for the purpose of proselytising.

One of the most significant changes over the past forty years has been the redefining of family, embracing single parents, same sex couples, and blended and gathered families. Families now include not only those directly related, but sometimes friends and colleagues. In addition, single adult households are on the increase and likely to increase with an ageing population and more flexible relationships. In the Hebrew Scriptures, families were known as households involving not only blood relations but often concubines, slaves, and other female partners of the patriarch. Children raised in the family were not only those of the married couple. The traditional Christian view of marriage as between a man and a woman is now challenged by same-sex couples, and the roles of women and men in relationships have been shifting for some time.

In earlier Christian times, marriage was often only for the well-off and to protect inheritance. Sexual relations between couples, previously reserved for marriage and procreation, is now for many simply a pleasurable activity with no relationship consequences. There is now greater participation of women in the Australian workforce, the age of formal/legal marriage continues to climb, women as well as men are taking responsibility for the care of children and lifestyle expectations are shaping time management and values. All of these changes challenge the Church's influence on families. The '#MeToo' and the 'Black Lives Matter' movements have also raised serious cultural challenges in community values and attitudes. Likewise, the Covid pandemic has seen shifts in attitudes to community life.

What is occurring with these changes is a shift in the broad cultural context of faith in the public arena, with Christian faith viewed as personal rather than public, commodified and secondary to the needs of the modern state with economics as the emerging god. The Covid pandemic that emerged in 2020, however, has raised serious questions about this agenda and challenged the view that humanity has the capacity to set its agenda alone. The pandemic has created havoc around ideological views of all persuasions but in particular the idea that the state should play a minimal role regarding a market economy, the governing of resources and individual rights and freedoms. In Australia, at both Federal and State levels, Governments – at least in the short term – have loosened, if not abandoned, economic principles previously held as sacred to stimulate economic recovery.

As Church and Christians, discipleship calls us to engage in all aspects of life that impinge on the Creation. Nourished by tradition and Scripture, there is opportunity here for the Church to be a robust and passionate advocate for a better world, enhanced by the gifts science has brought to the fulfilling of God's Creation, proclaiming and building the Kingdom of God. There is the place for cooperation with those who do not share a faith perspective but who likewise seek the common good.

To engage in the public forum, in the space of ideas, is therefore to recognise the disturbing spirit of God not only in the Church but beyond. Have not the revelations of the abuse of children in the Church and other institutions been a reminder to the churches that God is not controlled or limited to the Church? Is this not an example of the disturbing spirit of God, prompting the question, what else may this spirit be calling us to do? How does faith in the crucified and risen Christ open our hearts and minds to our failures, to be faithful and to restore our confidence in sharing the Good News?

The Church is not immune from criticism. We do not have, as Archbishop Desmond Tutu says in his book *God is not a*

Christian, a monopoly over morality. Morality has been seen to be lacking throughout the history of Christendom. Such criticism is not limited to church leadership alone. Politicians, the police, lawyers, the military and other community groups have also been criticised for similar failures. The Church is seen as an easy target, however, and has received consistent and regular criticism partially due to the high moral standards it constantly preaches but has failed to exercise. It is refreshing to hear the voice of Pope Francis on these matters as they relate to the Catholic Church. His words to the Roman Curia in December 2019 on discernment and courage reflect a new approach to the challenges of the time:

> Here we must be aware of being tempted to assume a position of rigidity. The rigidity that comes from fear of change and ends up disseminating limitations and obstacles on the terrain of the common good, turning it into a minefield of incomprehension and hatred. Let us always remember that behind rigidity lies some imbalance, a vicious circle. Rigidity and imbalance feed each other.

The question Robert Fitzgerald asked when he was president of ACOSS, at a Melbourne City Mission staff symposium in the late 1990s, of whose side the community sector was on is, I suggest, one that churches need to address. Fitzgerald asked: was it that of the government, the agency or the poor? This is the same question I continue to ask of faith-based agencies as they appear to rush into more contracts and grow larger. Who are they called to serve: their own privilege or the cries of the people?

The amendments to the *Marriage Act* in 2019 to allow same-sex marriage is a further example of how far the community has moved from orthodox and traditional church teaching. This has encouraged some parts of the Church to shout out and claim that their religious freedom is being eroded and that there should be greater protection for people of Christian faith. This claim stands at odds with those same voices wishing to sideline and discriminate against other faiths and their practices while demanding privilege for themselves. While it is important to respect the rights of those who disagree, this is not the same as saying that anyone who criticises should be denied their rights, as some voices demanding greater religious protection in the Church are suggesting. Christian faith as a prophetic faith in the marketplace of ideas needs to be concerned not about its own privileged position, or of an image that challenges the perceived wisdom of economics or social order but, as Miroslav Volf writes, 'being an instrument of human flourishing, in this life and the next'.[2]

---

[2] Miroslav Volf, *A Public Faith*, Grand Rapids, MO: Brazos Press, 2011.

4

Justice

BREAKING OPEN THE WORD OF GOD for our times remains both controversial and challenging. How one reads and understands Scripture is a source of major conflict and disagreement, not only among biblical scholars but more importantly for religious leaders who wish to hang on to past dogma as final and without the need for interpretation in today's context. I draw attention to this fact for two reasons. First, how one reads Scripture is a significant if not the major cause of division within and between traditions and denominations. The second reason is to name the discrimination that exists in the church.

My ministry has always been on the edge of the Church's mission although I have always understood it to be the core of the teachings of Jesus. Throughout my ministry, the call to justice for all has often received more criticism from within Christian circles, while being supported by many others without faith in the broader community. For many years, I was labelled and regarded by sections of the Anglican Church, including bishops, as merely an ordained social worker, especially by those who regard the Church's primary purpose as proselytising, and regard service to the disadvantaged as charity, and of secondary importance.

This stands in stark contrast to the call of the prophets of the Hebrew Scriptures and the teachings of Jesus. To love God and yet discriminate, ignore or blame those who differ – the poor and the disadvantaged – remains wrong, both theologically and biblically.

My introduction to justice and the prophetic voice of mission was not so much from the pulpit or church teaching but through the actions of individuals and contact with the welfare agencies. Even my own life experiences of meeting and engaging with people struggling through life brought the needs of others constantly to my thoughts. These experiences were important in grounding my own understanding of the full meaning of mission. Listening to the stories of others can be both profoundly moving and challenging. Sadly, these opportunities seem lacking today. Local people engaged in voluntary work as part of their Christian commitment and speakers who came and preached on Sundays introduced me to the agencies of the church and their work among the poor. This was common in Anglican circles at the time.

Initiatives to engage the poor, care for the homeless were driven not by any central church command or diocesan policy but by parishes and individuals, clergy and lay people working on the edge of society and committed to a discipleship of service to others. They were often sidelined and ignored by church leadership. These initiatives led to the establishment of the agencies of today, many of which were originally parish outreach programs. Many of the early philanthropists of the day had a strong sense of Christian duty and established and funded the work of charity from their own resources and without the support of their governing body.

Now a line is often present between the agencies of the Anglican Church and the diocesan authorities. The agencies are not present as participating or voting members of the General Synod other than as elected individuals by their own dioceses. In many places, evangelism, perhaps better described as proselytising, is seen as the primary Christian agenda, with justice and service to others a secondary concern. In my own spiritual and faith journey, the Cross symbolises for me the essence of faith, to love God and to love your neighbour, especially those who are different, dissident or difficult. This viewpoint challenges the Prosperity Gospel of the more evangelical and parachurch groups. Their teachings are at odds with the teachings and parables of Jesus in each of the Gospels.

Dorothy Lee speaks about four elements of the call to wholeness and the implications for the mission of justice and social responsibility. In Mark's Gospel, the question of suffering and evil is explored; in Mathew, fear and anxiety; in John, the quest for meanings; and in Luke, divine purpose. I suggest that each of these has to be an element of the Church's participation and mission in the public square.

Mission embraces proclamation, adoration and service. The Christian narrative is diminished when mission ignores any one of these, especially the call to be for 'the other'. God is ever present in the world, seeking justice truth and hope for those diminished and struggling, calling the Church to account and standing alongside in times of joy and tragedy. Our task is to stand beside God. God is already at work and we are to discover where and how to join God's mission for the world. When, as Christians, we fail to share our wealth, skills and resources, our own redemption is diminished.

5

Justice and the Anglican Tradition

NLIKE THE ROMAN CATHOLIC CHURCH, the Anglican tradition does not have a codified set of law, dogma or teaching clearly setting out policies and principles, unless one sees the 39 Articles of Religion in the *Book of Common Prayer* in this way. I suspect for most Anglicans this is not the case. This is in part due to the nature of the Anglican Communion and reflects its diverse nature and lack of a central magisterium. Anglicanism is marked by the decentralisation of authority and diversity in prayer and worship. This is not to say that there is no social teaching, only that it is likely to vary across dioceses and nations. A person will have a perspective on what the Scriptures teach and how they should be expressed and acted upon in the present.

What may be considered a form of social teaching for Anglicans, at least over the past 150 years, can be traced to the cleric F. D. Maurice and the Christian Socialist movement in the United Kingdom in the mid-nineteenth century. It should be noted that his approach to social issues was pragmatic, a vehicle to achieve certain goals, theological or ideological. Maurice was not a social revolutionary but rather believed that a new order would rise when the laboring classes would take their place in reasserting the foundations of society as seen in the ministry, life, death and resurrection of Jesus. Consistent principles, however, were hard to find. Like others of his time, Maurice differed in his approach to specific issues, self-help on the one hand and government intervention on the other.

Perhaps similar approaches can be seen today. Alan Wilkinson claims that Maurice and others who were the leaders of the Christian Socialist movement of the times arose as a response to possible revolution, poverty and inequality. These early stirrings encouraged others, such as Henry Scott Holland and Charles Gore in the 1880s, to come to the scene. The twentieth century saw William Temple influential in the post-war welfare state, followed by a variety of followers working in the East End of London, including Kenneth Leech and David Hope.

Some would argue that Britain as a colonial power articulated a social and political agenda of subservience and exploitation in the name of the Christian God during its time of imperial expansion and domination; and there is some truth in this. But in Australia, Anglicans since the time of the First Fleet have played active and significant roles in working with and among some of the most disadvantaged and excluded people in the Australian community, first as chaplains and moral exponents of the Christian faith to prisoners, soldiers and free settlers of the first settlements. The prisoners in particular were victims of poverty and duress, many transported for petty crimes and leaving behind friends and family. Later, Bishop Burgman in Canberra, known as the red bishop and described by many as standing in the tradition of Maurice, expressed strong views about privilege and justice.

At the international level, Archbishop Desmond Tutu has for over forty years been a tireless exponent of a Christian understanding of justice, challenging both the churches and the global community. He has been an outspoken critic of apartheid in South Africa and of injustices elsewhere. I recall Desmond Tutu addressing a gathering of over 2000 young people in St Paul's Cathedral Melbourne, without notes and with passion. He held the students present in the palm of his hand for over fifty minutes and answered their questions honestly, admitting that the churches have got many things wrong, and encouraged them to speak up about injustices. Many of Tutu's social and theological positions are at odds with other Anglican Church leaders, and in particular those who are members of GAFCON, the bishops' movement opposing the Lambeth Conference.

In recent times, a new approach appears to be emerging to address global issues, internal church divisions and how to use the media in a constructive way. This has been demonstrated by Justin Welby, Archbishop of Canterbury, and Pope Francis. Both speak with a sense of humility and openness to dialogue and engagement with others, though they are not without their critics from within the churches. The recent support by Pope Francis for recognition of civil unions for those of the same sex was one issue that stirred criticism – although his stance has recently been modified in relation to marriage.

In 1937, Bishop Burgmann, Anglican Bishop of Canberra and Goulburn, stirred the conscience of the Australian nation and his brother bishops in the Church of England (as it was known at the time) when he spoke about his dream for a great Australian nation:

> There is one way and one way only to save the drift and that is by giving the people of Australia a vision of the Christian faith recreating the social order in this new land; leaving behind the bitterness of the old world with its class hatreds and its international rivalries; establishing justice

in economic fields and inspiring political action to great creative endeavors. The Christian faith did this once for Europe when it tamed barbarians and sustained a vision of unity for the whole continent. The Christian faith is still as vital and as relevant as it ever was as is to Europe, but the churches must forget most of the things which now obsess them and be caught by a vision of the work to be done.[3]

The commitment to justice by Anglicans in Australia has been defined by a set of broad Christian principles and by theological engagement in specific issues. The Brotherhood of St Lawrence in Melbourne has concerned itself with structural reform of the Australian economy, including a sustainable income and public housing provision. Agencies that are members of Anglicare Australia are active in promoting the best care for children and their families, as well as a wide range of other services that address domestic violence, child abuse, disability and the aged. The approach to these issues in the beginning relied upon the insights and the commitment of individuals who braved the established nature of the Church of England in Australia. Burgman was scathing of the establishment nature of the church of his time:

> It is the business of the church to minister to sick and neurotic souls [yet] it ends up far too often, with these fearful, neurotic souls in the saddle so far as the institution is concerned. [...] The church has failed to bear witness to international justice as she has failed to bear witness to justice in inter-class relations. As her failure in the latter case produced communism, so her failure in the former has given us Nazism and fascism. [...] Churches are always

---

[3] See Peter Hempenstall, 'An Anglican Strategy for Social Responsibility: The Burgmann Solution', in John Moses (ed.) *Anglican Social Strategies from Burgmann to the Present*, St Lucia: Broughton Press 1989.

a danger to religion. They get interested in themselves, in their own ground in aggrandisement and power, and countless things that keep them too busy to live closely to the life of the people. [...] Churchman get interested in the world beyond this world, largely to escape the trouble setting right the wrongs that afflict the human race.[4]

Others who followed in Burgman's footsteps were Sister Esther of the Community of the Holy Name, Father Tucker of the BSL fame, Bishop Geoffrey Sambell, David Scott, Peter Hollingworth, Alan Nichols and Sister Kate, and numerous others who challenged both church and community to address disadvantage. Most of these spokespeople understood their ministry as being in the broader community and not limited to the faithful. Their comments were not always supported or understood by other religious leaders across their traditions.

Central to those mentioned above was that they based their theological understanding of what it means to be human on the 'word made flesh', with the Church's task to spell out and implement God's deep passion for the Creation, the Kingdom of God. In the birth of the Christ-child, God entered into our humanity, not in a pretend way but fully. As Luke proclaims, he is both the suffering servant of God and Messiah. His message is to the gentiles, the agnostics, the doubters, the renegades, the unbelievers. Today, God remains with us in our trial and tribulations, feeling our despair and hurts, yet always calling us to new possibilities. The birth of the Christ-child is affirmation of our humanity – a risk taken by God, a foretaste of a world that could be, if we lived according to his principles of justice and love, a kingdom or community where God is sovereign and where people are created in the image of God, as one who is

---

[4] Ibid.

compassionate, forgiving, merciful and generous. Sadly, there were those within the Church of England at the time of Maurice who were dismayed and alarmed at what Maurice and his contemporaries did, believing strongly in social inequality as divinely ordained. One had to accept one's place in life, as F.D. Maurice suggests:

> So long as the working man-maintained order and decorum and kept the peace and observed the law of the land, and was a respectable member of the community, so long as he felt satisfied the working man would meet with the sympathy and approval of those in order of providence who were placed in a higher and another position in life.

William Temple sought to respond to the criticism of his times of this emerging and prevailing social comment by church leaders by emphasising that Christians should exercise their moral responsibilities in a Christ-like spirit, exercise their civil rights in a Christian spirit, and critique those that offended Christian principles. He went onto say that the Church should not always offer solutions to the problems but raise the level of debate. This response by Temple provides a template for a constructive role for the Christian in today's contemporary Australia, but it requires ownership of a new set of guidelines that I outline later in this book.

In my own lifetime, the Church of which I am a member did play a mediating role on social issues, with regular engagement and comments from bishops and their welfare agencies. This is now in rapid decline, as stated earlier. In a later chapter, I will examine further how the agencies of the churches should seek to reconnect with both community advocates for change and the more traditional church parishes including the establishment on new forms of faith community including joint ecumenical ventures.

6

The Prophets

I F WE ARE TO effectively find a voice for the churches in the public domain, a good place to start is the prophets of the Old Testament. They spell out a courageous agenda that speaks into the context of the day, voicing their anxieties and frustrations with the behaviour of both leaders and people. The prophets insist that God has made a covenant with his people and joined them in their search for justice for the outcast and needy. The prophets upheld the rights of the widow and orphan and appealed to the rich and powerful to be generous and responsive to those in need.

It is the stark contrast between the luxury of the rich and the misery of the poor that is Amos' concern. He was the first prophet to pronounce judgment on the whole of Israel. According to Amos, Israel flounders because its communal life does not live up to God's dream and hopes for the creation. God desires neither self-interest nor religious self-righteousness but rather denounces their behaviour and prophesies doom, because of their failure to observe the covenant.

The Book of Isaiah, as we have received it, is actually three books that have been edited into one. The first book, chapters 1–39, comes from the eighth century BC. Here the prophet speaks to the kings and powerbrokers of the day – the priests, princes, scribes and others. He criticised the corruption and abuses of his time, often made in the name of God, and challenged them all to do better. He called for them to reject the idols of money and power, the other gods, and return to the God of their ancestors. Here again we read how the leaders and people have a responsibly to act with justice and to live in harmony and to share their God-given resources.

The second part of Isaiah, chapters 40–55, dates to the exile in Babylon sometime during the sixth century BC and the third book, chapters 56–66, around the late fifth century. These later additions shift direction to God acting in history. Isaiah is one of the most quoted books in the New Testament and has contributed to shaping the direction of faith from the days of the early Christians.

Isaiah has a particular concern for the 'the oppressed, the orphan and the widow'. In Isaiah 28, the prophet speaks to the leaders of the people of Judah, particularly those with wealth and social privilege. The priests and other prophets are also identified as being not concerned with the poor and neglecting their responsibilities to ensure the wellbeing of their community. Exclusion is denounced, and here, as in other places in the text, excessive drinking and rich foods are associated with the exploitation of others in the community caused through unjust policies and practices.

Here, in our community, the same challenges are present and the Church needs to use its prophetic voice. Those in particular need – the homeless, the elderly, those with a disability, the unemployed and destitute – need preferential treatment and recognition, not be abused, ignored or forgotten because they lack a voice. The churches have accumulated wealth including property and assets over their time here in Australia. This wealth has been contributed by faithful men and women and has been used to create communities of faith, to build schools, welfare and other outreach programs. But in recent years they have become a symbol of privilege, such as with private schools. This raises questions about whether or not churches should continue to be sponsoring facilities that do not enable full participation by all members of the community. How does the wealth and power of churches intersect with their broader mission in our community today? How might we seek to speak to this reality and pressure for change?

Isaiah's cry for justice is expanded in chapter 32. Here, justice and righteousness are seen together, as they do frequently throughout the Scriptures, and are to be understood as two sides of the same coin. They are the characteristics that should define the nature and mission of the community of faith.

Isaiah proclaims with great emphasis that it is the poor with whom we are to share our lives and bounty. For today's Church, this does not mean merely giving donations for worthy causes. While this is important and a sign of commitment, especially when as individuals and even as churches it is difficult to address many causes directly, the engagement must go further and include structural reform of our economy. This is to ensure all are cared for and enabled to live a full and satisfying life. We should stop using discriminatory and labelling language such as 'lifters and leaners' and embrace a positive and hopeful agenda that cares for all humanity.

In chapter 32, Isaiah also rants about fools and villains who distort the truth. The prophet's point is that you cannot pursue justice if you cannot distinguish between good and evil. This challenge was faced by Nicodemus who came to Jesus by night but found the demands too much. This is common sense, but sadly not well demonstrated at many different levels in our community. This has been evident during the Corona virus pandemic, with people who should know better openly disregarding expert advice. The churches did act with integrity, setting an example by suspending all corporate gatherings including worship and committing themselves to staying engaged through phone, email, and personal support to those in need.

Like Isaiah, Micah viewed idolatry and injustice as the cause of God's impending judgment. For Micah the poor and oppressed are righteous and the rich the enemy of God. Jeremiah stands in the same tradition. He denounced the kings, judges, prophets, priests, rich merchants and officials of the state, in the context of the approaching Babylonian threat.

From this brief discussion of the role of prophecy, we are given the tools and objectives to engage in discussion and dialogue. The churches' tasks are to know the difference between good and evil, and to work together to build relationships with those who differ from us and who are affected by the impact of our decisions. As we reflect on the writings of the prophets, it is clearly not sufficient to sit back and turn a blind eye to the abuses, exploitation and failures of our community. It can be done; and the pandemic of 2020 has shown how many governments across the world can abandon neoliberal ideology to ensure the safety and wellbeing of all citizens.

Isaiah 42 is shaped by the exile in Babylon. When Israel was a nation, justice was demanded of all and administered by the King, but in Babylon there is no mechanism for justice and God raises a prophet as servant to champion it. The servant represents an ideal, a model for us today as both individuals and Church, and points to service not privilege as the key to building the Kingdom of God in today's context. The challenge here is to promote servanthood in a community that increasingly rejects Christian faith. Desmond Tutu, Mother

Teresa and Martin Luther King are examples of prophetic and servant leadership. But not everyone needs to reach celebrity status – all who are followers of Christ have been given the capacity to live their lives in the same way.

The last part of the Book of Isaiah is thought to have been written when Israel had returned from exile around 539 BCE. The emphasis became on covenant not only among the faithful but for all nations and races. The lesson for today is that no-one should be excluded from the life of the Christian community.

7

Justice and Moses and Jesus

OW MUCH DO WE KNOW about the society in which Jesus grew up in and lived his life? We know he was a Jew. He lived on the margins of Galilean society, far removed from the centre of religious and economic power. In his ministry, he was open to a wide range of people with a preference or deep concern for all those on the margins. He attended the synagogue; he went around preaching, healing and proclaiming the Good News. His own family were regularly challenged and amazed and he placed his followers – those who responded to his ministry – above family. He did not have a microphone, computer or access to the internet or social media. He told by story and lived as he preached. He used symbols that were well known, and conflict was a key element in his ministry. He moved out of the safety of the temple and synagogue into the byways and lanes of the towns and countryside.

What sort of society did all this take place in and how did it affect the way he spoke, the way he acted, his relationships with family and friends, his expectations and hope? In other words, how did he exercise his leadership? I want to suggest that how one views society and the world we live in will reflect how justice, grace, compassion is viewed. It is often said at funerals that how one understands death will shape how one understand life. If the divine does not exist in any way, then death is the end and there are no musts to how you should live. This is not to say an individual who does not confess faith has no principles, but they are more likely to show concern for the self.

Influential theologian Reinhold Niebuhr suggests that Jesus provided ideals, the 'impossible possibility' of loving our neighbours and forgiving seventy times seven. In entering the real world of politics and personal egos, he says the best we can hope for is a kind of 'rough justice'. But Jesus called for more than this.

Jesus spoke to powerbrokers, in language challenging their power and responsibilities in the exercise of leadership, both in the religious and political establishments. A similar voice is needed today. The ruling and political classes seem unable to provide for those who struggle to support their families, and regularly chastise them for needing assistance.

The search for meaning is central to the teachings of Jesus. Who are we and what is our purpose? Jesus spent time in the wilderness at the beginning of his ministry. This defined his ministry. This search for meaning is a deep, personal and communal journey for everyone, although it is true to say that it is not always recognised or acknowledged. The current wilderness time the Church is experiencing is an opportunity to redefine our mission as God's mission. How can we find meaning when we are different to others, or our understanding of faith challenges orthodoxy? John's Jesus speaks to this in these words, 'All things came into being through him and without him not one thing came into being' (John 1:3). What has come into being in him was life. Life embraces meaning and the call to be an agent of God's unconditional love and hope. As Dorothy Lee says, 'We are not talking about the light of the sun, but the illumination of humankind and what it means to be human'. Jesus is the revealed Son of God, bearer of unconditional love of the creator that enables us and calls us to do likewise.

The Hebrew Scriptures contain many references to God's dealings with the world, from the stories of Creation through the accounts of the patriarchs, including the covenants with Abraham and Moses, the Exodus, the giving of the Law, the establishment of the monarchy, the Exile and the era of the Second Temple. All these accounts give us a narrative of God's justice, of God's dealings with the world and its people. These accounts, along with the Psalms, the Prophets and books like Ecclesiastes and Job provide us with – as Walter Brueggemann writes – a coherent picture of God's nature and identity as one of justice and hope. Brueggemann writes in *The Practice of Prophetic Imagination*:

> In the context of Israel's completed testimony, it is difficult to overstate the pivotal importance for the rest of Israel's testimony of (...) the commitment of Yahweh [and of Israel] to justice. If we consider in turn the prophetic, psalmic, sapiential and apocalyptic texts, it seems evident that Israel, everywhere and without exhaustion, is preoccupied with the agenda of justice that is rooted in the character and resolve of Yahweh. This justice to be rooted in Yahweh, moreover, is to be enacted and implemented concretely in human practice.[5]

Uncertainty and fear are widespread across our world, not only on account of the Covid 19 pandemic but for nearly 2 billion people in war-torn areas, those affected by drought,

---

[5] Walter Brueggemann, *The Practice of Prophetic Imagination: Preaching an Emancipating Word*, Minneapolis: Fortress Press, 2012.

others governed by corrupt or dictatorial regimes and who struggle to feed their families. In Australia, over 2 million individuals, many with family responsibilities, are affected by violence, lack of an adequate income, and health issues including serious mental illness. Equally, fear is increasingly embedded in our culture.

Fear, however, can bring us closer to God as we reflect on God's awe, love and justice. In Matthew 11, in what must be one of the most beautiful texts of the Gospel, Jesus bares his soul: he speaks of his unique relationship to the Father and of the Father's deep desire to embrace us in our weakness and weariness. The passage records one of the most intense moments in the life of Jesus. This is one of the few insights we have of the interior feelings of Jesus with his disciples, but we do witness a lot of what he does. We see the relationship with his Father turned into action.

Jesus moves and speaks in public spaces, healing and standing with and alongside those on the outside. He teaches, he feeds, challenges, forgives and speaks in prayer. His religion and faith are not limited to the private but is very public. He stands beside those who struggle, the ungodly, the unbeliever, the exploiters and greedy, the outcasts and sinners and here beside them he shares the Father's heart and soul. They are encouraging words. Jesus, the miracle worker, the scourge of demons, invites us to lean on him and learn from him, for he is gentle and humble of heart. This invitation is to be shared with all humanity and is to be an expression of God's enduring presence. They are wisdom moments of hope and compassion that teach us much about human living. The most effective witness to God's justice and love is to demonstrate the story of Jesus, the great Christian narrative as our story, embedded in our individual lives. It is this that defines and separates us from the broader secular and humanist community.

This whole theme of justice is further cemented in the book of Deuteronomy in a sermon spoken by Moses. This follows God revealing himself in a burning bush to Moses while he was tending his father-in-law's flock near Horeb, the mountain of God. God commissions Moses to help free the Hebrews from Egypt, the land of oppression. (See Exodus 3:1 to 4:17 and Exodus 12:37 to 14:4.) They finally leave Egypt to experience a long time in the wilderness on their journey to the promised land. Moses endures the moaning, groaning and complaints of the Hebrews. He ensures their wellbeing (Exodus 15:22–17:17) and in Exodus 19 committed the people to observe the commandments of God communicated to him during a 40-day stay on the mountain. This theology expressed in the book of Exodus is the basis and theological framework for the life and witness of Israel. It maintains that God is just and the source of all justice.

In a booklet written in 1990 entitled *Alongside the Poor*, Jesuit Andrew Hamilton describes the Israelites at the time of Moses as refugee workers, without rights and identity. When he called them out of Egypt, God made them a people. So, the Exodus story was God's alliance with the poor. When strangers sought asylum among the Israelites, they were to remember how they themselves had been saved as strangers, and to welcome them generously. The year of jubilee, when debts were set aside, ensured that the division between rich and poor was mitigated over time. Furthermore, this was not simply a matter of pious exhortation; it was written into their laws.

The questions that automatically follow from such claims are these: Is God just? Is God always just?

- Ask a gay person.
- Ask someone with a terminal illness.
- Ask those affected by a natural disaster.
- Ask a feminist.
- Ask those in postcolonial countries.
- Ask a victim of domestic and or patriarchal violence.
- Ask someone who has experienced spiritual and psychological control.

Is God equally the God of the torturer as the tortured? Is God equally the God of the victim and the perpetrator? Is God equally the God of the exploiter and the exploited? Is God the God of the CEO who gives himself a huge rise but denies wage justice to others? Can God be held accountable for things that go wrong or are there other factors at work? If so, what are those other factors? When friends and others raise such questions, how do you respond? If tragedy and disappointment has struck in your own life, how do you answer the question? How do we respond to those who name themselves as Christian but distort the meaning of Scripture demanding lifestyles and belief consistent with theirs and theirs alone?

These are important questions that need to be addressed, and the churches need to provide answers and hope in each of these contexts. This must involve the whole of the people of God and must be first and foremost in the mind of our leadership and theologians. The answers need to reflect the unconditional love and grace of God and embrace the times and the world in which we live today. We must also right the wrongs of doctrinal error and embrace a way forward that liberates the human condition from meaninglessness and a sense of despair. There is also the need to find ways of hearing the voices of our respected theologians. Their books and lectures cannot be limited to the academy but must embrace broad prophecy and public discourse, accessible to all.

8

The Decline of the Church's Prophetic Voice

> The opportunity and claim of the Christian Church to make its voice heard in matters of politics and economics is widely resented, even by those who are Christian in personal belief and in devoted practice.

WILLIAM TEMPLE WROTE the above words in November 1941 when he was Archbishop of Canterbury and when the Church of England was central to public life in the United Kingdom. They were spoken at a time when the Church of England, as the established church, was actively involved in influencing and shaping much of British civil society, with the bishop and local vicar respected and embedded in community life.

The Anglican Church in Australia, although not an established church, has played a similar role in the public domain (but not to the same extent as in the United Kingdom). In addition, churchmen were present in the public service, led corporations, taught in schools, and were doctors, university staff, lawyers, judges and present in many other aspects of community life. Their influence on society has substantially declined, as Christian faith for many people is no longer central to their own meaning and purpose. The Gospel parables of the Good Samaritan and the Prodigal Son, along with the Sermon on the Mount, are distant memories for many. While they may have been important in shaping society in previous years, they are not taken as absolutes today, nor to have social and economic policy implications. In more recent times, the Church's role and voice has been diminished most notably in by being excluded from providing religious education in public schools. The words of Temple resonate even more strongly today.

Journalists, academics and writers of opinion pieces, along with increasing numbers of community members, see the Christian message and the Church as relics of a past era, speaking on matters from an historical and ethical perspective that is ignorant of the advances in science and technology that have improved the lives of millions of people across the world. (As previously noted, they fail to understand that much of secular and humanist thought and philosophy have their roots in Christian faith.)

Critics claim that in many areas of ethics, the churches' power and influence have restricted personal liberty and caused a great deal of hurt and pain, particularly in the area of personal morality, including gender roles, and individual equality and freedom. Commentators such as the late Christopher Hitchens, Catherine Deveney, David Marr, Philip Adams and Richard Dawkins see religion and belief in God as the cause of much evil in today's world, inflicting on many people guilt and bondage, limiting creativity and stifling open debate on matters of human sexuality, rights, freedom and pleasure. To them, religion is seen and understood as naïve belief leading to terror and destruction.

This is a claim that has some validity but ignores the fact that Christian faith is not the only culprit in restricting personal liberty. Political regimes have and still act in ways that diminish the human spirit and freedom, and the critics of religion do not comment with such fury on these other aspects of power. (I need to add at this point that their criticisms of religion bear no resemblance to my understanding of God and the Christian narrative.)

In a different way, defiant and abusive comments that seek to debunk faith by outrageous comedy sketches, social media comments and acts of sacrilege have also increased in recent times, reflecting a growing antagonism towards any religious belief and often portraying believers as hypocrites and loonies.

This level of scepticism and disbelief in God have been fuelled recently by people of faith, for example Israel Folau's sacking by Rugby Australia for condemning publicly same-sex relationships and homosexuality in general. His statement has influenced the growing debates in this country over religious freedom and free speech, as has tennis great Margaret Court, now a pastor at a church in Perth, with her views on homosexuality. Their voices have been added to by conservative politicians and commentators of a fundamentalist religious viewpoint. These voices often express derogatory and even discriminatory comments about other faiths while demanding protection for themselves.

These debates have seriously eroded the message of the Gospels. Folau and Court are entitled to their views but they should not be presented as the only Christian position. Do we not all have an obligation to respectfully engage in discussion and public debate, accepting the democratic principle to acknowledge difference without resorting to abusive language and personal viciousness?

Similarly, and from my personal perspective and experience, leadership in the Church has not always been exercised with tolerance and respect. There has been a failure to listen, employing consistent, unsubstantiated attacks on those who fail to live up to or accept the moral teachings they espouse as the 'Christian way', and therefore religion has been given a bad name. Douglas John Hall explains it this way:

> [T]he threats of which I am thinking include not only terrorism and counter terrorism but economic injustice and the misdistribution of global resources, environmental degradation, the oppression of women and children, global encircling diseases, and the many other impediments to creaturely wellbeing that use and misuse the religious impulse for their inspiration. The day is over when 'religion' could be thought of as an unambiguously Good Thing, as many in the past believed it to be. Informed and sensitive members of every faith tradition today are likely to think twice, if not explicitly to demur, when they hear themselves described as a 'religious person'.[6]

This has led and enabled politicians and others who in past years refrained from challenging religious leaders in the public arena to become critical and at times patronising.

I recall Philip Ruddock, when he was Minister for Immigration, in the mid-1990s, criticising leaders of faith-based agencies in Melbourne. In a discussion about boat people, asylum seekers and refugees, he chastised the gathered leaders of these organisations, of which I was one, telling those gathered that if it weren't for the churches and their agencies, there would be no debate on the government's policies towards asylum seekers. The rest of the nation was not interested or concerned, he claimed. Community attitudes to refugees has softened over the past few years, but insufficiently for the federal government to act humanely and with justice towards asylum seekers.

---

[6] Douglas John Hall, *Waiting for Gospel: An Appeal to the Dispirited Remnants of Protestant 'Establishment'* , Eugene, OR: Cascade Books, 2016.

Likewise, Alexander Downer, when he was foreign minister, described clerics as seekers of

> cheap headlines and are remarkably vague and uncertain about matters which their faith should teach them with certitude, but remarkably certain and dogmatic on matters of considerable complexity and ambiguity about which they have no practical experience.[7]

Further, a leading economist, when challenged about free market economics during a debate, when the GST was being opposed by church agencies, said that I should not worry, as my job and the agency were safe. He saw that the agency's role was to pick up the fallout from the 'market'. Neoliberal free market economics is now the politically acceptable approach for political parties of the left or right.

In this area, the Church, including many of its own agencies, has been silent, offering little if any comment or critique of an economic paradigm that devalues the role of government enterprise in favour of the private. On the other hand, a range of new, non-religious organisations have emerged, leading and engaging in the debates once led by the welfare agencies of the Church.

The complexity of the issues facing the community – such as climate change, short term employment, housing and health care shortfalls – seem to be beyond understanding, comprehension and without ready solutions; and are in a sense overwhelming. The left of politics seems to have abandoned its traditional base while the right no longer takes responsibility for those in need. As a result, anger surfaces across communities, and the flamboyant and colourful –

---

[7] Reported in the *Sydney Morning Herald*, 28 August 2003.

often with less than desirable policies and lies and half-truths – become attractive, gaining the support of those who feel deceived, exploited and ignored by mainstream political leaders and parties.

Substance in discussion and debate on many matters of economic and social policy is often absent and is reflected in political leaders being able to dismiss the Church when it does comment. A better strategy for the Church in areas where it may lack knowledge or skills is for the leadership to draw on the wealth of experiences in the agencies and in individual Christians who in their own professional arena are experts in areas such as economics, the environment, public transport and the alleviation of poverty. This would be a good example of shared Christian leadership. In the 1980s, unemployment in Australia was not easily understood and the unemployed were much maligned and regularly described as 'dole bludgers'. This started to change when agencies such as St Vincent de Paul helped highlight the anxiety and pain of the unemployed.

The churches, including many of the agencies associated with the Church, know they have failed on many occasions and have been corrupted and seduced by power and privilege. This recognition, however, should be a starting point for greater Church engagement in the public forum, not merely on theological matters but on other, broader issues. My reading of the Gospels clearly shows Jesus not bound by the Temple but in the community where he taught and healed. In the pandemic of 2020, the churches have been forced to refocus much of their activities, not only from prayer and worship but to their connections and presence in community life. This can only be a good thing for community engagement and restoring the image of Christianity.

9

The Churches' Vocation of Social Justice

There is no longer Jew or Greek, there is no longer slave or free, there is no longer male and female, for you are all one in Christ Jesus (Galatians 3:28).

THESE WORDS, WRITTEN BY SAINT PAUL 2,000 years ago, are central to the Christian faith. They speak of a vocation for the universal and point to an ethic of social justice and solidarity. The Christian tradition's account of the humble circumstances of the birth of Jesus, represented in the nativity scene, is in the same spirit, identifying Christ with the marginal, the maligned and the poor.

In an article in the *Guardian* newspaper of December 2019, this quote from Scripture was used to introduce an article on the struggle for the soul of Christianity. It went on to discuss how people of faith were themselves divided on many of the social and ethical issues of today; and also how increasing numbers were depressed about how religion was being used by many political leaders to support the abandonment of these principles.

The commitment to human rights irrespective of gender, race or sexuality, embraced in the Pauline text, is having to be fought all over again. What we are seeing at the present time is an attempt to twist, distort and rewrite the message of the Gospels in a way that cloaks faith in religious language while promoting bigotry and denying the references to Jesus feeding the hungry, healing the sick and clothing the naked. Instead, the accumulation of power and wealth has become the essence of this rewriting of the Gospel message to give comfort to those who think otherwise. As already mentioned, this is the emergence of the Prosperity Gospel.

Prayer is an important element in the life of a Christian. However, so often it is misunderstood. Prayer is often used to 'fill the gaps' when all else fails or during times of crisis. This understanding of prayer is not the full story. Prayer also involves personal and corporate action. Principally asking for God to intervene without any responsibility of our own is irresponsible and lacks integrity on our part, and is a failure to address the wrongs that have occurred by our own actions. If drought persists in some parts of a country, there is also the need to ask why. What part did our failure to treat water and climate in a different way play? If we see no role for the individual, then God cannot be understood as always just, loving or compassionate, but, rather, discriminatory and unjust.

The narrow if naïve view of prayer has been challenged by an increasingly intelligent community and is also rejected by many Christian leaders who understand prayer and faith in a wider context. In the context of the 2020 pandemic, prayer for our health and research workers expressed a universal hope that solutions would be found and encouragement for those who were seeking a vaccine to work in harmony and to cooperate. It is not God's fault that political leaders failed to hear the cries of those affected. Prayer is not just about asking, but also involves action, standing with and alongside those in need, respect for the environment and a commitment to act on the part of the Creation and humanity. It is a recognition that humanity is in partnership with the divine to work towards the fulfilment of Creation, as Saint Paul says in his letter to the Romans 8:39.

It was pleasing that at Christmas 2019 a number of religious leaders spoke in a prophetic and passionate way on issues of climate change, respectful dialogue and the voices of young people who joined the call. Sadly, the engagement of the students was dismissed by political opponents of climate change and told to go back to school. However, these matters resonated with the wider community and received cover in mainstream media. This suggests that the community expects to hear from religious leaders on crucial matters that impact on life. In 2020, some coverage by mainstream media to voices from the churches on issues that were being experienced from the pandemic were highlighted in news reports and print.

10

How the Church Can Speak in Context

WHAT I HAVE ATTEMPTED to outline briefly so far is why the Church's influence has waned, and why at the same time our nation's commitment to care for our neighbour also appears to be floundering. Why is it that we appear to have abandoned values that helped create and shape our nation and are now on a different course when it comes to compassion and justice?

This is starkly evidenced by the lack of concern for the 70 million stateless people across the globe, and for individuals affected by unemployment here in Australia. In the past, did religious belief establish in our community life a sense of compassion and justice that now no longer sees expression in our political leaders and the wider community? On the other hand, political leaders who do express commitment to Christian faith regularly distort, even corrupt, the text and teachings of Jesus to support their own ideological and political ambitions. In this agenda, they have co-opted people of faith. This occurred during the lifetime of Jesus. Religious leaders were complicit with the state in order to protect their privilege.

Denial, revenge and self-interest alongside erratic political behavior have become what is expected. Is this the reason behind our refusal as a nation to support the needs of asylum seekers and refugees, forgetting the facts about our own confiscation and ownership of this nation from the first inhabitants? Have the past thirty-five years of free market economics with the emphasis on self permeated our values and identity to such an extent that we cannot see beyond the immediate and the self? It appears that the churches have been seduced by the voice of self-interest, exemplified by their failure to name and shame the reasons for increasing numbers of children living in poverty in single parent families, by growing income disparity between the rich and poor, the lack of public housing, the reduction in foreign aid and the need for refugees to be treated well.

I make no apology for this statement. The churches have in many ways abandoned their mission to proclaim the values of the Kingdom of God, to identify the structures and values that limit human growth, and to challenge self-interest.

This leads me to suggest and reiterate at this point that traditional approaches by the churches in speaking into the public forum need to be rethought and new ways explored. Churches are diverse in doctrine and challenges between conservatives, liberals, progressives and traditionalists contribute to a failure to be heard by the wider community. Even where there is agreement, such as on the needs for asylum seekers and refugees, powerful media owners drown out the voices of reason and faith. Choosing when to speak and in what forum is essential in ensuring the message is heard. During the 2020 pandemic, many Christians voiced their disappointment and felt let down by leaders who they expected to deliver life-affirming public statements amid the closure of churches even for individual private prayer. Little was heard in mainstream media for the reasons noted earlier.

Mainstream churches, along with many of their agencies, have failed to read the times with sensitivity. In addition, there is a lack of reasoned and theological debate on key issues, with the voices of theologians absent. The big picture and the highest of hopes of what it means to be human need to be addressed more rigorously. At times, the best contribution of the churches may be to moderate or facilitate discussion on the key issues that affect community life. This will require the churches to respect differences among themselves while engaging with the wider community. Respectful dialogue and conversation must become the order of the day.

The prophets of the Old Testament spoke into the context of their day, denouncing bondage and slavery to the powerbrokers. They spoke loudly and clearly, even if they were sometimes ignored. While those within the Church who challenge the powerbrokers of today, naming the 'elephants in the room', are often ridiculed, they are not alone. Voices other than those of Christian faith suffer also in the same way. Christians are called to engage with pain and suffering, abuse and exploitation not only from a distance, nor from the comfort of our lounge chair or in a passive mode, but in an active and life-changing manner.

This means going where it is most difficult, unpopular and challenging. In practice, it means standing with the homeless, the asylum seeker, the abused and violated, the outcast and rejected. It is the place of the Cross. In his book *Faith in the Public Square*, Rowan Williams argues strongly for a renewed engagement by the Church with society. He says, 'The Christian faith is not a matter of vague philosophy but of unremitting challenge to what we think we know about human beings and their destiny'.[8]

Standing with those who find themselves alone in the gutter of despair and without hope can be a challenging experience because it gives a sense of reality. There's a story from the Holocaust that illustrates this point. An old man was digging out a filthy latrine as a Nazi guard stood over him. The guard said to the old man, 'Now, where is your God?' The old man replied, 'Right here in the muck with me'.

Rowan Williams' comments affirm that the Christian faith does have something profound to say about the human condition. But churches need, as a matter of priority, to acknowledge that the Christian Church is no longer the stakeholder but one of many stakeholders in Western societies, in seeking to win the hearts and minds of people and to share an ethic for living. The challenge then is to examine ourselves and to get our own house in order if we are to speak with credibility and integrity into the culture of the day. It is more likely, I suggest, that our witness will be enhanced and the Christian narrative will be taken more seriously when we address our own failures as churches.

Brian Trainor[9] speaks in a similar vein when he argues for a more active and decisive engagement of faith with the secular state. He suggests that the secular state and the wider community need the churches to remind them of the deeper and personal dimensions, including ritual, needed to enhance the wellbeing of its citizens. Like Williams and Miroslav Volf, Trainor opposes the growing view that the future should be

---

[8] Rowan Williams, *Faith in the Public Square*, London: Bloomsbury Publishing, 2012.

[9] Brian Trainor, *Sacred Precedes Secular: Why the State needs the Church*, Melbourne: Mosaic Press.

determined by the human race alone and without any influence of religious belief. The broader task here is to adjudicate or mediate between the various cultural and religious traditions to seek the common threads for the building of a more just society.

For Christians, the ethic of God's purpose for the Creation exemplified in the life, death, ministry and resurrection of Jesus, provides a solid and vibrant code for relationships and belonging. In Matthew's Sermon on the Mount, the ethic for building the Kingdom of God is not about rule keeping for the sake of order but must come from one's inner self. It is not simply about learning a set of ethics but more about identity and inner sacredness.

This poses a number of questions. Is the Church's relevance today a response only to its own behaviour? Have we been too preoccupied with ourselves and our own survival as an institution, ignoring the cries of others? Or is the Christian call so radical to the empires of today and the antithesis to power and corruption that the challenges facing us are overwhelming?

This is, as I have been suggesting, another reason why Christian faith is in decline. Christian faith is no longer about the radical alternative but instead has become too much like the secular and humanist. Are we as people of faith increasingly seen as presenting to the public arena a vision of Christian faith that is narrow, lacking a real sense of the presence, and a lack of depth in our own understanding of the Christian narrative? Does the Church rely too much on selected texts that ignore the reasons for the poor and dispirited? Why are we afraid of addressing and speaking out on structural reform and embracing shared resources? Our bias for the poor and oppressed, however, as Henri Nouwen says, is where the voice of the crucified one will be heard, and faith restored. Nouwen writes,

> Those who are marginal in the world are central in the Church, and that is how it is supposed to be! Thus, we are called as members of the Church to keep going to the margins of our society. The homeless, the starving, parentless children, people with AIDs, our emotionally disturbed brothers and sisters – they require our attention. We can trust that when we reach out with all our energy in the margins of our society, we will discover that petty disagreements, fruitless debates and paralysing rivalries will recede and gradually vanish. The Church will always be renewed when our attention shifts from ourselves to those who need our care. The blessing of Jesus always comes to us through the poor. The most remarkable experience of those who work with the poor is that, in the end, the poor give more than they receive.[10]

In contrast to the absolute statements made by those who claim leadership in the Church today, Jesus rarely gave a straight or expected answer to a question. His response to the religious and political leaders in the context of the day defied logic and rationale in their eyes. He spoke in parables and metaphors that the people of the day understood, but not the powerful and religious. He challenged their understanding of God's identity and purpose and made them feel uncomfortable. While they frowned, the crowds followed, even if they often failed to get the centrality of his teachings.

In Chapter 6 of John's Gospel, the crowd is looking for Jesus. He has just fed them, as described earlier in John with the feeding of the 5000. Now they are hungry again. They find him

---

[10] Henri J. M. Nouwen, *Bread for the Journey: A Daybook of Wisdom and Faith,* San Francisco: Harper, 1997.

on the other side of the sea. He figures out they are hungry again and challenges them to seek not for food that sustains the moment but what really matters, to recognise and believe in the gift of life that has been given by God, a more enduring food that requires engagement, responsibility and action. More than the immediate. The message here is simple: what we believe should shape how we live.

Writing on the Church's decline in influencing the Western world, Douglas John Hall suggests that the life-changing message of the early church to ordinary people is what made it influential. He says,

> Christianity, as faith centered in Jesus, as the Christ came to be called, got a foothold in the world, and a vital and vocal minority changed the world, because it proclaimed a message that awakened men and women to possibilities for human life that they either lost or never entertained.[11]

Hall goes on to say that the established churches 'are prevented and inhibited from proclaiming the gospel precisely on account of their establishment, or the remnants of the same'. They have become part of the political elite embracing wealth and power. They appear at times to have little understanding of contemporary life. Perhaps one of the reasons for a growth in religious fundamentalism is due not only to the failure of political leadership that enhances the wellbeing of some at the expense of many but also due to what I described earlier as Prosperity religion, the idea that belief in Jesus and accepting him as saviour and Lord brings with it the promise of all doing well. This approach to Christian faith is reinforced not only by political leaders but also celebrities seeking favour and support.

---

[11] Douglas John Hall, *Waiting for Gospel: An Appeal to the Dispirited Remnants of Protestant 'Establishment'*, Eugene, OR: Cascade Books, 2016.

It should be called out as both a sham and manipulative. It is a misrepresentation of the Gospel narrative.

How do we counter the voice of those who sell religion as a sign of God's providence and promote prosperity as an outcome of belief with the call of the prophets of the Old Testament and the Gospels that speak about the building of the Kingdom or reign of God? The emphasis on discipleship is not about me but the other. It is not about creating God in our own image but rather, as the prophet Micah claims, 'What does the Lord require of you, but to do justice, to love kindness and to walk humbly with your God' (Micah 6:8). Compassion for the poor and justice for all is not a sideline activity for Christian activism nor is it a trickle-down donation to those in need but central to building a just and compassionate community reflecting on the unconditional grace of God. The missionary task is not about money, status or wealth but about relationships.

The struggle of Jesus in the wilderness before he embraces the will of the Father provides a solid connection to the call of discipleship for our times. The missionary task is about how we care for those who are often struggling with life. It is not proselytising but service to the other that is central. The emphasis on the other cannot be dismissed or ignored by Christian people. Whenever we remain silent when evil, oppression and ignorance is expounded, we are in partnership with the evil doers. There is the urgent need to practise what is preached and to challenge those who claim faith but whose lifestyle and wealth accumulation suggest otherwise.

The reality of the loss of influence of Christendom is not fully understood or appreciated in many places in the mainstream churches who refuse to listen, engage, and study. There is a longing for the past without any recognition that we cannot go back. Many Christians have been 'seduced by the spoils' and, like other previously respected and even revered institutions, accepted many aspects of the prevailing empire. On occasions, there is the failure to recognise what their engagement may bring to the debates and that there are those in the parishes and congregations waiting to hear from them even if they may disagree. At other times, when responding to challenges and criticisms, church leadership appears to be unaware of how their words are read and interpreted. Both spoken and written words are often not read as compassionate, open to dialogue or even gracious. Instead, they are interpreted as hard line and closed. This is not only about style. Statements on forgiveness, reconciliation and restoration are regularly rejected in favour of revenge and retribution.

The Christian message of love, forgiveness and tolerance towards the other is now a voice crying in the wilderness, as Brueggemann and others have stated, and requires new ground rules, clear expectations and conversation on all sides. A renewed and revised commitment to the prophetic voice of Christianity is urgently needed, and negative responses to the churches' engagement should not act as a deterrent.

11

Reclaiming a Prophetic Voice

O ONE OF THE MOST CRITICAL ISSUES, then, to be faced in re-establishing a prophetic calling and participation in the public forum as primary mission and evangelism is to begin with the Church itself and review how it engages with the wider community, including its own governance, accountability, transparency and decision-making. The first task, then, is for the Church to speak to itself, even to include a wide-ranging audit of its life to ensure that it is listening. This needs to involve a commitment to renewed ecumenism and stronger connections with the social justice arms of the churches.

The loss of a strong ecumenical voice by the National Council of Churches and local state bodies has helped marginalise both the denominational and broad-church response and allowed parachurch associations like the Australian Christian Lobby to fill the space occupied previously by the mainstream churches. While the ACL may be a loud voice, it does not represent the mainstream churches but rather the more fundamentalist and Pentecostal denominations. Their success in the public arena is a result of many factors, including a united media strategy, funding of media as the core business of ministry and mission, skilled spokespersons and active lay person involvement.

Urgent action is required by the mainstream churches to resource and strengthen the various ecumenical and multifaith bodies to address the challenges. The selection and engagement of key lay people like Stephen Duckett from the Grattan Institute in Melbourne in the areas of healthcare is also important. There are many issues that the churches agree upon, and these should be the first line of engagement.

The fact that mainstream media no longer have religious affairs journalists means that mistakes and misinterpretation are common. This creates a dilemma for churches who wish to speak into the public forum and who are prepared to enter into dialogue and conversation. Church leaders who have attempted to speak are regularly ignored; and articles rejected by journalists ignorant of religion. What is required is experienced journalists with faith to be employed by the churches. If this is not possible, then at least journalists with skill and an ethic equal to that of the churches should be engaged. This is likely to mean the need for the reprioritisation of traditional ministry tools and resourcing.

How then are the churches to be a moderating influence on debates and conversations on social and economic issues within our churches and with the wider community, including our political leaders? How does one address the one-minute grab? Despite the context that the Church finds itself in, religion and faith are not irrelevant to the modern world. Rather, there is a challenge to find new ways of speaking, not as the only stakeholder but as one of many stakeholders in the dialogue. This requires skills beyond preaching, and the use of places and spaces where secular Australians are to be found, such as the shopping mall. Rather than building new churches, we should be renting space within a shopping mall. One example of this approach would be to locate within an opportunity shop or similar establishment a worship and hospitality space to meet and greet with those who visit.

There is also a wealth of talent and skills in congregations This is a matter all of us who exercise leadership, not only in the Anglican Church of Australia but all churches, need to give more attention to, especially where the knowledge and resources are available for a more informed view on the ethical and social issues presented. The churches have a variety of expertise and resources available to them, but its ecclesiastical structures and the separation of entities restrict a more informed response.

While bishops remain central to the life of churches, they are not the Church. Increasingly, in my own experience and others, lay people no longer simply accept the view of the local bishop or moderator; and the influence of agencies and lay members has risen. Diversity in views and ideas within faith traditions should be valued and encouraged, not restricted, ignored or even forbidden by ecclesiastical structures. Current ecclesiastical power should be balanced, with proper lay responsibility and governance that reflects a true participatory form of leadership. There should be a commitment to shared leadership within the priesthood of all believers that acknowledges and embraces the skills of all members of the community of faith.

In Australia, it has been agencies of the churches that have been the regular and constant advocates on matters of justice in recent years. On occasions, archbishops and moderators have spoken on such matters as gambling, foreign aid, and asylum seekers, but it has been the agencies and a small number of prophetically active parishes that have borne the responsibility for social comment, advocacy and action. These same bodies have resourced heads of churches in this task. Social responsibility committees and public affairs committees have been the other source of public comment, but in recent years most have been starved of funds and bishops often appear reluctant or reticent to use the advice and the resources of the agencies or committees.

I speak from over thirty-five years' experience of ministry, although there were exceptions. I recall at least two major issues where the archbishop of the day requested that I speak as chair of the Melbourne Social Responsibilities Committee on dying with dignity proposals and the introduction of poker machines in Victoria. One of the most poignant occasions of the influence of an Anglican archbishop was when Keith Rayner spoke at an anti-gambling rally on the banks of the Yarra River. He began his address with a prayer, 'As Jesus wept over Jerusalem, so we gather to weep over Melbourne' (or very similar words), which made it onto the front page of the newspapers.

A distinctive Christian response to the social and economic issues facing Australia today will require more rigorous attention to detail and a vision that goes beyond the immediate to future generations. Further, it requires ongoing theological and biblical reflections on Scripture and the relationship between science and faith. This should start in parishes, be resourced by theologians with the primary goal of education for all on how to speak into the public forum. The lockdowns in Victoria as a result of Covid 19 have seen theological colleges open up their teaching to a wider range of audiences by their web and streaming options, in order to address key social, ethical and economic issues. This is a welcome initiative that should continue in the future as a means of sharing knowledge. The establishment of the University of Divinity, formerly the Melbourne College of Divinity, is another example of promise for greater engagement by theologians to encourage community debate that is not limited by denominational control. Likewise, the Centre for Christianity and Culture, although limited by its Canberra focus.

Speaking into the public forum is mission, a commitment to reflecting Christ's mission to the world, a mission that is vigorous, vibrant and prophetic. As Rowan Williams says, we need to recover a sense of 'convergent belief in the possibility of liberation from the systems of violent struggle, in a way that genuinely opens doors in our world'. The question for the Church, as I keep saying, is how the Gospel can be presented in this rapidly changing global scene as well as at the local level here in Australia. How may Christ and the Kingdom of God, incorporating the values of heaven for the here and now, be taken seriously and with integrity in this world of neoliberalism and free market economics? We need a model of using the world's resources that does not rely on the trickle-down effect to assist those in most need, nor increases the wealth of the wealthy and powerful.

A glimpse of such a possibility began to emerge during the 2020 Covid 19 pandemic. A new global ethic needs to be discovered or rediscovered that seeks to share the resources of the earth in an equitable and just manner, an ethic of justice for all that is central to the teachings of the prophets and the ministry of Jesus. An ethic that honours compassion, mercy, sharing, and the gift of life.

12

Where to Now?

A troubled soul asked God, why do you not feed the hungry? In the silence that followed, God's word resounded, why did you not? – Helder Camara

I HAVE OUTLINED many of the changes that have taken place over the past fifty years in Australia. These changes have and will continue to impact on church and broader Christian values in ways not previously experienced. There are no readymade solutions. The suggestion that we return to traditionally held views including a patriarchal and structured church is not the answer. Rather, a deeper commitment to the unconditional love of God, the central ethic of faith, is required. Additionally, the Christian narrative or story that has framed the traditional doctrines of the churches now urgently needs to emphasise the history of the formation of Scripture, the purpose envisaged by its writers, the place of myth and legend and the necessity of interpretation. In fact, this may mean different interpretations as each of us bring our own thoughts, experiences and wisdom to the table.

It should be remembered that when we speak of the authority of Scripture, we need also to recall that the Canon of Scripture we call the Bible was put together in the fourth century by a group of bishops for both political and religious reasons. As Karl Barth once said, 'the Bible is the inspired word of God but subject to the actions and views of scholars and religious political leaders'. Throughout the Church's history, it has been interpreted in different ways, often leading to breakaway groups. To demand that those who do not agree leave the Church because of a different opinion and approach to Scripture is arrogant and lacks any notion of God's grace. The Church is the people, not only bishops and clergy. Christians do not worship the Bible, but Jesus the Lord. To approach Scripture without taking into account the context of the times and the customs of the day is to diminish its status.

Patriarchy must be replaced by new forms of governance that embrace what it means to be the Body of Christ and not simply another institution, not for profit, but rather expresses in its own life the love of God that liberates. Leadership needs to be more clearly focused on service and not control; care and not management. Political lobby groups and methodology need to be abandoned and replaced with shared discussion and an openness to disagree.

Previous expectations on how to proclaim the Kingdom of God will not prevail, nor will the voice of the Church be a given. The community is better educated, multicultural, multi-faith and demanding accountability and justice when things go wrong. The Church is also confronted with rising costs and regulation that will follow the Royal Commission into Institutional Responses to Child Sexual Abuse. Diversity of viewpoints on doctrine and ethics, management styles, inter-church relationships and leadership are now also under constant challenge. All of these issues impact on the voice of the churches in Australian society today and are the catalyst for finding new ways of being church and speaking into the public space. Informed laity and community members are often better informed on ethical and social issues than the clergy. Likewise, theological education is primarily now not for those who seek ordination but for the wider community.

Jonathan Sacks, former Chief Rabbi of London, speaks about the rapid return to tribalism across the globe and asks the question: surely no just God would condemn innocent people as they go about their daily business? What place then does Christianity have in our contemporary, multi-faith and increasingly secular society? Is there a place for a Christian ethic that underpins our search as a nation and as individuals to fulfil our human potential? I am suggesting that despite the shifts in society and the challenges to the Christian ethical base, the answer is yes.

If the answer is yes, then the Church and Christians must do some serious reflection, not only on understanding society but also traditional doctrines and teachings on matters of personal ethics and community life. Recent statements by both the Roman Catholic and Anglican Archbishops of Sydney show the depth to which they will go to preserve their doctrinal tradition, verging, I suggest, on Donatism, with the Anglican Archbishop stating homosexuality is a sin, and condemning same-sex marriage. Both archbishops are entitled to their views, but they are not the Church and their views are at odds with increasing numbers of Christians and others who have long left behind these hierarchical and patriarchal viewpoints. I am suggesting that now is the time for a radical overhaul of how the Church is governed and who should exercise leadership.

The view on same-sex marriage mentioned above is a clear example of how church leadership fails to understand the context, including the emerging knowledge from science and psychology on the nature of the human person. Instead, they continue to speak with an authority that has long been rejected, particularly in Western societies. Hiding behind privilege and power and sacred texts as absolutes will not be the way to promote the Christian narrative. Jesus challenged the religious authorities of his day by his words of welcome and grace. Is this not the way for today? He sought to open their minds and hearts to the revelation of God in his own life and times.

Speaking and participating in the public square is mission. At the heart of mission is wisdom, wisdom that Paul reminds us is folly to the world but is stronger and wiser than all human endeavours (1 Corinthians 3:19). Wisdom is not to be understood as knowledge alone, but rather how we are called to live in relationship to the whole of the created order, including our personal relationships with our fellows. It is wisdom of the highest order that embraces all that is noble, self-sacrificing, and devoid of self, what the Church has to offer a broken and fractured world. It is wisdom expressed in our service to others, understanding who they are and the challenges they face, just as Christ served those who were the outsiders, the despised, the prostitutes and the tax collectors. He spoke of grace while the religious authorities spoke about judgment. It is a reminder not to confuse morality with wisdom.

The history of the Church shows clearly its failures to be Christ-like and wise, and rather its tendency to play the political, ecclesial power games with great vigour, always at the expense of those who disagreed. We seem to be in a similar place today, although the Church no longer has an army of crusaders. Given the diversity of the Church in Australia, it is unlikely that consensus on all issues will be possible, nor may this be desirable. As a minimum, a vision of ministry and engagement with Australian society should include the following:

- an understanding that the sacred and the divine are grounded in our very being, both as individuals and the wider creation;
- a commitment to love and service to others as core Christian teaching, as exemplified in the Sermon on the Mount and the parables of Jesus;
- a recognition and affirmation that agencies and parishes are called to make a real difference to the lives of individuals and the communities in which they are located;
- a commitment to the value of research and community living alongside Scripture and the traditions of the Church;
- a willingness to take risks and to acknowledge that our own salvation is diminished when we fail to heed the cry of the other;
- a preparedness to listen to the voice of the faithful and those without Christian faith as they journey through life;
- a willingness to share leadership on matters of justice with like-minded individuals and organisations;
- a recognition that good works, charity and benevolence, while admirable in their intent, are symptoms of disadvantage and brokenness. Challenging the structures of the society that limit, diminish or exploit requires perseverance and advocacy;
- a willingness to share the pain and the brokenness of the world, acknowledging the presence of the Divine in the midst of human suffering;
- a willingness to be open to the disturbing spirit of God in the Church's own life and in the community;

- a willingness to acknowledge a journey of inquiry that embraces not only traditional religious doctrine but also different aspects of reality including science;
- an acceptance and recognition that the stories we have been told may not always be the right ones or even relevant.

How then does the Church reconnect with community? How do Christians exercise leadership at all levels of the Church's life, in the areas of teaching and community building?

As outlined previously, the world at home and abroad has changed. Today's urban communities can be described as high speed, high octane, nonstop, credit fuelled, technology-driven and shaped, market-driven, multicultural, multi-faith and on the move globally. It is estimated that 70 million people are stateless. How then is the Church to respond and what is its calling in this changing context? Where is constructive and respectful dialogue and conversation between believers and non-believers?

Our model of church still remains feudal in structure and clerical. Morale among clergy and laypeople is in many places low and our confidence sapped. We are divided in many ways, not least in the manner of how we read Scripture, how we worship, and our relationship with others. Even to speak of 'the Church' is misleading.

Our model of Church needs to change and adapt to the context and community of which it seeks to influence and engage while holding fast to the claims of God's kingdom as witnessed in the life of Jesus. There is no single way forward and experimental strategies will need to be involved, whether in a rural or urban setting. It is not just belief that is essential but how we live and give witness to the community in which we find ourselves that is demanded.

The assumption I am working on is that all who are engaged in ministry, proclaiming the Gospel, sharing the Scriptures and acting as loving agents of the other believe in the future of the Church and the Creation. And it is not our Church but God's Church. God will no doubt have something to say about the topic as well.

13

Challenges

THROUGHOUT THIS NARRATIVE, I have outlined the first challenge. It is the challenge to the Church to rethink and respond to the current context with greater integrity and to acknowledge the part it has played in shaping society's attitudes to faith and the Christian community. I have already mentioned that some of the Church's previously voiced views and attitudes need to be rethought. On matters of justice, governance, transparency and prophetic teaching, we need to speak to ourselves as well as the wider community. We are, in many ways, both part of the problem and the solution.

The Church in Australia is one of, if not the largest, employers in the country. Through its network of schools, colleges, universities, welfare, hospitals and parishes it employs many thousands of people from all walks of life. How do we model best employment practice, given our role and responsibility? Does our Christian belief stand as the foundation of our work, or have other principles replaced the need to ensure a safe and professional environment? How do we safeguard family life within our work practices? Why do we continue to discriminate against those whom Jesus himself would have connected with and engaged? Are our governance structures open and accountable? Why should the Church and its agencies be exempted from all forms of legislation that prevents discrimination and exploitation, other than perhaps those that require ordination?

Other issues the Church needs to address include population growth, human sexuality, and climate change. There is the need, as Walter Brueggemann says, to re-engage and to redefine our role as a stakeholder in the community, not as the only stakeholder but one of many. Do we live as Church and as Christians the vision of radical discipleship, of a society without fear and abuse? Is our Christian adherence compatible with our lifestyle? While recognising there is no single way to respond to culture, Brueggemann identifies the following as a way forward:

1. Take the present seriously and acknowledge our part in creating the present.
2. Identify the causes of the present challenges facing the community and name them publicly.
3. Acknowledge that we may not be able to reverse trends in either the short or long term.
4. Recognise our own loss of identity and acceptance.
5. Immerse and equip ourselves in the issues of the day with data and information for action, evaluating the options.[12]

Brueggemann goes on to say that central to all these approaches is the need to reclaim our passion for God and a voice to lead into a new realm where how we relate to one another and to God becomes the core business of mission. He affirms that the core of faith is the ethical question to embrace God's justice as the ultimate expression of God's unconditional love and grace, and that relationships are key to this expression,

---

[12] Walter Brueggemann, *The Practice of Prophetic Imagination: Preaching an Emancipating Word*, Minneapolis: Fortress Press, 2012.

as found in the teachings of Jesus and the Old Testament prophets. This means a greater willingness to partner with others and not seek privilege as a community of interest but a community meeting need. The Church should challenge any society that sees Christian faith as simply another commodity or institution, but, as I have said previously, speak about itself as the 'Body of Christ'. The first need is both to address our past actions, judgments and failures with lamentation; and ensure they do not occur in the future. This requires better accountability and governance structures at all levels. It involves lessening the power of clericalism and including lay people with real authority and engagement, not simply as advisors.

The second challenge is to engage in an urgent discussion on the meaning and future shape of civil society. Many of the institutions of our times that have helped sustain and provide guidance are increasingly being shunned or challenged, not least the Church. Others include the professions, the parliaments and the law. Although the controversy of recent years in the United Kingdom concerning phone hacking has brought to the surface certain practices of media owners, the media in general reports to no-one, claiming immunity as a free press essential to a democracy. Lindsay Tanner, former Finance Minister in the Rudd Governemnt, for one, argues that the media is interested in a sensational quick word and opinion rather than reporting facts and engaging in bipartisan dialogue and discussion.

Debates in the Federal parliament in recent times have often been no more than personal attacks on the integrity of individuals, and sometimes controlled distribution of details in key policy areas has been restricted. The exposure of a range of alleged sexual assaults in parliament has intensified scrutiny from the media of the urgent need for cultural change not only in Parliament buildings but the wider community. The growth in continuous TV news coverage and the steady decline in print journalism is contributing to a further dumbing down of public discussion. Challenges to the public broadcaster by commercial media owners and politicians is a major threat to both media objectivity and impartial broadcasting but also to democracy itself.

While it is true that new forms of social media may help to address the challenge and improve discussion, there is little evidence to suggest that this is helping to modify the propaganda and bias coming from major Australian newspapers. There is also the arrival or recognition of 'fake news', partly driven and accessible with social media and propagated by some politicians to suit their own political agenda. How the churches use media and communication to assist their mission requires a stronger commitment and resourcing of strategies that will provide an alternative voice to political rogues and social activists peddling false and fake news. The Covid pandemic has shown the churches responding in many creative ways to engage and worship, unreported by the mainstream media. New platforms and acceptance of new ways of being church have arisen. The challenge is not to revert to the parish feudal model as the only means of proclamation, adoration and service. There is little doubt that many churches will continue to live stream worship as a means of outreach but to meet the needs of an ageing community.

The third challenge for the churches and the agencies is to increase their own level of research in order to inform themselves when a Christian approach is likely to differ, and to engage in discussion that is more than about their own privilege or position. We need to recognise that the Church's view may be countercultural; however, this should not mean that the churches cannot affirm where Christian values are still present widely or be comfortable with difference. Building relationships with the universities and think-tanks such as the Australia Institute and The Centre for Christianity and Culture is one way of doing this, and will enable cheap criticism of the Church's mission to be debunked and raise the level of the Church's contribution to social and economic policy.

An example of the Church bringing an alternative viewpoint to the table for the wider benefit of society was the joint report, in April 2009, entitled 'Building Financial Health and Wellbeing for Disadvantaged Australians in the Wake of the Global Crisis' by Anglicare Australia, Catholic Social Services Australia, Uniting Care Australia and the Salvation Army, which provided the necessary data for the federal government to accept the advice of the networks and provide urgent funds to protect the most vulnerable in the community. The report highlighted the additional costs that would occur if support were not forthcoming.

The most profound challenges – as I have already noted – the churches face is how we deal with significant differences in matters of personal morality, including human sexuality, euthanasia and the role and shape of the family. Miroslav Volf speaks about this when he explains that future dialogue on these matters will come not from the centre but from the margins and from listening to where people are hurting or struggling. He goes on to say that this does not mean accommodating the world for 'today's whims are tomorrow's old hats'. It does, however, mean that we need to rethink our approach to the use and understanding of Scripture and the formulation of human-constructed doctrine.

The fourth challenge is global urbanisation and the need to address growing income disparity and demands for energy. While Victoria speaks about building an $8-10 billion tunnel, the rest of the state misses out on infrastructure and more young people leave rural homes and move to our increasing larger metropolitan cities. In many places in rural Australia, it is the Church that stays, although under great duress. What other institution has a presence in every community, and how well do we use this existence to enhance mission? How many of our parish communities have outreach programs that connect with their local community other than fulfilling the Church's own existence? Here I am thinking of a range of community services, such as loneliness support, drop-in meals, financial assistance, accommodation and like-minded services to combat the fragility and brokenness of many people. Think how better education, health, housing, overseas aid and transport could be if our approach to the future was less about urban growth and instead more about rural sustainability. The Covid virus situation has shown further the need for addressing these issues.

The fifth challenge is the rising costs of providing services at the local parish level while attendances decline, and goodwill is diminished. Increased regulation and administration costs legislated by governments, as well the costs of media, lay staff salaries and travel will continue to impact on mission at the local and national levels.

Goodwill among previous professional groups who often provided services *pro bono* is now virtually nonexistent. Unlike earlier times, clergy are well-paid when all the benefits and tax concessions are provided and a small parish with less than 100 worshippers requires $125-200,000 per year. The challenge for the Church is then to find ways of maintaining not only its existing structures, but also how to gain a presence in the new and expanding suburbs of the metropolitan cities and rural centres.

It is estimated that in Melbourne the cost of planting a new parish exceeds $3 million. The immediate implication is to prepare now for a changing demographic and presence. New models of presence need to be explored. The model of a Stipendary vicar, minister, pastor or priest in a parish will be challenging to maintain. Shared resources between two parishes are one option, while another could be the renting of community space for long periods. While this may not build up capital, it will enable easy movement as populations move and new communities are formed. It may also allow communities of faith to concentrate on mission and not maintenance.

A sixth challenge is the rapid decline in the public power base of the Church. I have alluded to this throughout. While some traditions still have significant influence in politics, the professions and many other aspects of society, there has been a rapid decline in others. In the Roman Catholic Church, while Mass attendance continues to decline, the outcomes of their education system ensure a cultural basis for the Church and a strong commitment to justice. This is not the case with Anglicans or other Protestant traditions. Both their membership and political influences continue to decline.

The seventh challenge is to recognise and acknowledge where the divine presence is at work outside the Church and for the Church to seek help from outside its own resources in order to strengthen its own mission and life. This should involve working in partnership with organisations with similar objectives, noting that it is God's mission not ours that is important and that the Christian narrative is God's. Christian faith may not provide all the answers to the social and ethical issues of the day. Neither should we assume the secular or humanist option is better. But as Church and Christians, we are called to engage in all aspects of life that impinge and affect the creation. Nourished by our own tradition, the opportunity is there for the Church to be a robust and passionate advocate for a better world while recognising the right of those who do not share a Christian faith perspective but who also seek the common good.

The foundation behind these issues for us as individual Christians and Church is to ask how we as people of faith can speak with integrity, transparency and in a prophetic way that transcends church politics, study the Scriptures with an open mind and as ongoing revelation, ask serious questions about our own privilege, listen to the voices of the oppressed and marginalised while challenging those with power and authority to act, in the words of the prophet Micah, 'to do justice, to love kindness and to walk humbly with your God' (Micah 6:8). This then is much more than simply quoting texts.

How then do we begin to do this task? As I have already said, it begins with being informed and particularly at the local and community level. This is where I suggest real opportunities are present, but it may mean ditching some existing priorities for new and risky ones. We need to spend time on our own journey of faith and not think we know it all, and from this see that which will enable us to speak with integrity, understanding and hope. As a Church, we must rediscover the central message of the Gospel, understand our context and continue our journey in hope and love in the wider and faith community. How do we seek to address the challenges and confusion of our times and rekindle, reimagine and reinvigorate our churches and faith communities? This remains the ultimate challenge.

In my own experience, sadly, too many Christians have not kept pace with the times and our knowledge of Scripture is often minimal. According to Luke's Gospel, when Jesus spoke in the synagogue, he was well versed in the Hebrew Scriptures and, on this occasion, he challenged with knowledge those he spoke to.

The young Swedish climate change activist Greta Thunberg came to mind as I reflected on Luke's Jesus and speaking to the gathered eclectic congregation from across the religious, political and economic spectrum. Her challenging, assertive, demanding and proactive words on the threat of climate change have been challenged, sidelined, avoided and ridiculed by many of our political leaders, social commentators and corporate executives. She has been described as naïve, simplistic and failing to understand the real world, as well as being manipulated by others.

Increasingly, we are hearing, from many different walks of life, the same or a similar assessment of Christianity. Followers or believers are described as believing in myth and a non-existent make-believe man in the sky, and conned by the Church. Like Jesus when he was challenged, and his parentage and community denigrated, this young woman and thousands of school children across the world demanding action are denigrated by the powerful and influential, who would prefer to run them out of any debate, even by threatening them with sanctions for speaking their minds prophetically. We may say that we are not like that, but I am also reminded of the saying that 'evil flourishes when good men and women remain silent'. I find it perplexing that our policy makers can provide relief for those affected by drought and fire but are unwilling to address the causes of such calamities, whether human made or otherwise.

Luke is aware of the needs of his own community and his writings are coloured by the conditions of his time. He recognised the need to make sense of the story of Jesus for the people of his generation. In his story there is hope of liberation from the oppression of his day so that they can truly become the people of God. Luke is offering his fellow believers and sojourners a robust resource to account for their faith in the dominant Greco-Roman culture of his day. It remains the challenge for us in our free market, neoliberal, secular context where economic growth is the mantra of the day to do the same.

On her 96th and last birthday, I asked my mother whether she could have ever envisaged the massive amount of change that had occurred in her lifetime. Her quick response was no. Likewise, I suggest that when we think about the future of Christian faith in Australia and the place of the Church, or should I say churches, the task is certainly unclear. I suspect also that we in the Church did not comprehend or see the distrust in the Church coming. But an informed faith is essential if the Church at the local, regional or national level is to be successfully engaged in the public space of policy and ideas.

Conclusions

I T SHOULD BE CLEAR that there is no single or easy way for the Christian faith to engage with the culture in which it is placed. Culture is complex, and faith can stand with or against it. In Western culture it is sometimes difficult to see a dividing line between Christian faith and the broader values expressed. In his book Public Faith, Miroslav Volf identifies important aspects of faith that are required to relate to the culture of the day:

1. a prophetic faith that seeks to mend the world
2. grace as a cornerstone of faith
3. a commitment to the other at all times
4. a reflective and transforming approach to engagement with the culture
5. witness that reflects belief and human flourishing
6. religious freedom and expression for other faiths.[13]

The words of Romero's Prayer reflect similar thoughts:

---

[13] Miroslav Volf, *A Public Faith*, Grand Rapids, MO: Brazos Press, 2011.

It helps now and then to step back and take the long view.
The Kingdom is not only beyond our efforts,
it is even beyond our vision.

We accomplish in our lifetime only a tiny fraction
of the magnificent enterprise that is God's work.
Nothing we do is complete,
which is another way of saying the Kingdom always lies beyond us.
No statement says all that could be said,
no prayer fully expresses our faith,
no confession brings perfection,
no pastoral visit brings wholeness.
No program accomplishes the Church's mission,
no set goals and objectives include everything.

This is what we are about.
We plant the seeds that one day will grow.
We water seeds already planted,
knowing that they hold future promise.
We lay the foundations that will need further development.
We provide yeast that produces effects far beyond our capabilities.

We cannot do everything
and there is a sense of liberation in realising that.
This enables us to do something and do it well.
It may be incomplete, but is a beginning, a step along the way,
an opportunity for the Lord's grace to enter and do the rest.
We may never see the end results,
but that is the difference between the master builder and the worker.

We are the workers, not the master builders,
ministers, not messiahs.
We are the prophets of a future not our own.

— Ken Untener[14]

---

[14] Ken Untener (1937–2004) was Bishop of Saginaw, USA.

In his teaching, Australian theologian Francis Moloney has described the Church as 'the broken and forgiven people of God'. Others describe the Church as the Body of Christ. Both these understandings stand in contrast to the usual description of companies, corporations, institutions and organisations with a legal entity. In any complex society like Australia, this requires speaking and acting in a way that is not disrespectful to another religious tradition but rather one that sees common ground and acknowledges difference. It requires sensitive and loving language, with attempts to stand in the shoes of those who have a different faith or none at all in order to gain a deeper insight into your neighbour's views. A generosity of spirit is required while remaining authentic to your own beliefs.

Church life and engagement with the communities of today are in transition. This, then, requires a long-term view of the future. Immediate resurrection for the churches as they have been is unlikely, particularly in the light of religious pluralism and increasing fundamentalism and religious initiated violence. This trend should be of major concern for all religious people, Christian or otherwise, as it distorts and provides simple answers to the complexity of human life.

In order to address this challenge, theological and biblical education in our churches is of the highest priority. Such education must grapple with the challenges of our times, speak with respect, engage in dialogue and seek a deeper understanding of other faith traditions. Bible studies have to be more than meetings to discuss text and should be linked with the world as it is and be open to interpretation.

An illustration of this is how we view the resurrection. For many Christians, resurrection only means what happens to them when they die. Equally, resurrection means the transformation of the world, the creation of God's rule and kingdom now. Likewise, the atonement is assumed to mean that our sins are forgiven, but it is also about a change of heart and policy, a different worldview.

Jesus' death transforms the world and sets in place the establishment of the Kingdom of God, the public reality of this kingdom is the fulfilment of heaven on earth. This understanding sets Christians apart from the secular world (though we must not forget that a great deal of what we call secular or humanist has its grounding in the Judeo-Christian tradition).

We may long for a romantic past (that, by the way, forgets the deprivation and tragedy of war, the lack of antibiotics, sewerage and adequate housing) where the Church was centre-stage in many places as not only the House of God but also the pinnacle of social life. Local cricket, tennis, football, scouts and guides and kindergartens were all commonplace community facilities attached to the local parish. This provided a natural way of connecting with the community. While church attendance was larger in those days, it was still only a smaller percentage, other than at Christmas and Easter, of those who utilised the facilities. Today, few churches provide the breadth of sporting and youth group activities. They are mainly the province of schools and councils. In reality, the provision of such facilities is beyond the financial capacity of the local church. Therefore, we need to find ways of connecting.

The key to this is leadership – leadership that embraces language that connects, stories that resonate, names the 'elephants in the room' with integrity, admits and acknowledges past failures, knows their audience, is respectful of difference and ideas, and is prepared to take risks even when they may be unpopular. Leadership needs to be aware of the framing story of our times that embraces science and technology and greater understandings of the complexity of human life across different parts of the world.

Leadership needs to embrace vison and hope for the future and not be tied down with administrative and management issues. Leadership that sits with and alongside those who are voiceless, the shamed, the confused, the refugee, and those unable to move forward on their life's journey. Leadership that takes the long-term view, acknowledges their own vulnerability and brokenness in light of the demands of the Gospel. A voice that recognises that there are limits to our abilities to change all we see as amiss and therefore prioritises. Leadership that embraces the wisdom of others, that is reflective of Christian mission, that is not limited to programs but rather living in relationship with all of God's Creation. Leadership that recognises privilege and status as a barrier to discipleship.

This is to embrace a new way of being Church where resources are placed in personal interaction, engagement with communities acknowledges their life struggles and search for meaning and purpose and does not dismiss their questioning. Leadership that seeks to empower the people of God in their relationships. Implicit in all these aspects of leadership is the ability to listen to dissent.

Bishop Peter Selby speaks about Jesus as the embodiment of divine love that regularly challenges our political systems and source of authority. Today, we are living in a world that has replaced divine authority with sovereign authority sanctioned by central banks, corporations and the powerful elite. In the same way, private media owners seek to control the political process by overriding the national and personal interest for the benefit of individuals rather than the community at large. This approach creates an illusion of satisfaction for those who benefit from such a means but discriminates against those who fail to live up to these values and struggle to survive. Leadership in our churches should be engaged in this debate with rigour, advocating theological principles that speak of stewardship, responsibility and equity, not only for those of Christian faith but for all people.

Democracy demands that the religiously motivated translate their concerns into universal rather than specifically religious actions. It requires that their proposals be subject to argument and amenable to reason, and if I seek to pass a law banning a practice, I cannot simply point to the teachings of my Church. I have to explain why, say, abortion violates some principle that is accessible to people of all faiths and those who have no faith. Why do we allow young men and women to go to war, possibly to be killed, or capital punishment to continue but oppose abortion?

This is going to be difficult for some who believe in the inerrancy of the Bible, as many evangelicals do. Within a pluralistic society, we have no choice. Politics depends on our ability to persuade each other of common aims based on a common reality. It involves compromise but religion does not always allow compromise. If God has spoken, then followers are expected to live up to God's edicts, regardless of the consequences. To base one's life on such uncompromising commitments may be blind, but to base our policy-making on such commitments would be dangerous.

A future public voice for the Churches must embrace the mission of the incarnate Jesus as loving , compassionate and generous to the other and to recognise sacred Scripture not as the focus of our worship but rather as the story of God's people throughout the times as understood in their context. As Mark Wingfield said in the *Baptist New Global Newsletter* in July 2019,

'Too much of Christianity is built upon absolute certainty and not enough on divine mystery'.

Dealing with difficult issues in the Church means being there for the long haul. It requires taking the long-term view and responding to the disturbing spirit of God for our times. As noted earlier, the Church is not responsible for all that has happened in our community life. Many of the challenges, like 24-hour, seven-day weeks, globalisation and terrorism, to name just three, are beyond its control. This realisation means that churches need to prioritise their actions and words to ensure their maximum impact. One final thought: we cannot do everything, and we are not the messiah or messiahs. The future of the life of the churches and the whole of Creation has to be entrusted to God. The future rests ultimately in God's hands and our task or mission in these in-between times is to remain faithful to the task at hand.

Bibliography

Walter Brueggemann, *The Practice of Prophetic Imagination: Preaching an Emancipating Word* (Minneapolis: Fortress Press, 2012)

Raymond L. Cleary in *The Church and Civil Society*, edited by Francis Sullivan and Sue Leppert (Adelaide: ATF Press, 2004)

Douglas John Hall, *Waiting for Gospel: An Appeal to the Dispirited Remnants of Protestant 'Establishment'* (Eugene, OR: Cascade Books, 2016)

Andrew Hamilton, *Alongside the Poor* (Melbourne: Victorian Council of Christian Education, 1990)

Peter Hempenstall, 'An Anglican Strategy for Social Responsibility: The Burgmann Solution', in *Anglican Social Strategies from Burgmann to the Present*, edited by John Moses (St Lucia: Broughton Press 1989)

Tom Holland, *Dominion*, (Little Brown, 2019)

Dorothy Lee, *The Gospel Speaks* (Mahwah, NJ: Paulist Press, 2017)

Henri J. M. Nouwen, *Bread for the Journey: A Daybook of Wisdom and Faith* (San Francisco: Harper, 1997)

R. Otzen, *Charity and Evangelization: The Melbourne City Mission 1885-1914*, PHD thesis (Department of History, University of Melbourne, 1986)

Oscar Romero, *Inspiring Quotes*, www.inspiringquotes.us

Jonathan Sacks, *Not in God's Name: Confronting Religious Violence* (London: Hodder and Stoughton, 2015)

Peter Selby, *Liberating God: Private Care and Public Struggle* (London: SPCK, 1983)

Lindsay Tanner, *Sideshow: Dumbing Down Democracy* (Melbourne: Scribe, 2012)

William Temple, *Christianity and the Social Order* (London: Pelican Books, 1941)

L. J. Tierney, 'The Church and Social Welfare: The Historical Background', unpublished paper delivered to the Victorian Council on Social Welfare, 1962

Brian Trainor, *Sacred Precedes Secular: Why the State needs the Church* (Melbourne: Mosaic Press)

Desmond Tutu, *God is not a Christian* (London: Rider, 2011)

Miroslav Volf, *A Public Faith* (Grand Rapids, MO: Brazos Press, 2011)

A. Wilkinson, *Christian Socialism: Scott Holland to Tony Blair* (London: SCM Press, 1998)

Rowan Williams, *Faith in the Public Square* (London: Bloomsbury Publishing, 2012)